MARRIAGE

VOWED INSEPARABLE

Raul Ries

SOMEBODY LOVES YOU ®

PUBLISHING

WWW.SOMEBODYLOVESYOU.COM

Carpenter's Son Publishing

Marriage: Vowed Inseparable

By Raul Ries
Copyright © 2019 by Somebody Loves You Publishing

Editor: Claire Wren

Cover Design: Donna McCartney and Rex Agagas

Requests for information should be addressed to:
Somebody Loves You Publishing
22324 Golden Springs Drive
Diamond Bar, CA 91765-2449
(800) 634-9165
mail@somebodylovesyou.com
www.somebodylovesyou.com

Library of Congress Cataloging-in-Publication Data
Library of Congress Control Number: 2015947914
Ries, Raul.
Marriage: Vowed Inseparable

ISBN: 9781949572803
1. Ries, Raul Andrew 2. Calvary Chapel—USA 3. Somebody Love You—USA—Evangelist—Radio 4. Marriage 5. Family 6. Singleness 7. Christian Living

CONTENTS

This book is a compilation of down-to-earth, heartfelt Bible studies given by Pastor Raul Ries from 1973–2020 to his congregation at Calvary Chapel West Covina, CA and at Calvary Chapel Golden Springs in Diamond Bar, CA.

Included in these chapters are excerpts from personal interviews with him, as well as his weekly leadership studies with his staff and meetings with local pastors. Minimal editing has been done in order to preserve the genuineness of his teachings as given.

DEDICATED TO

those couples who are struggling in their marriages.
My prayer and hope is that as you read this book, you
would come to know the original and amazing plan for
marriage that God ordained for man and woman in the
beginning—an inseparable union fashioned in the ages
before time was, to bless all those on earth, who would
unite in marital vows before Him.

May you come to know the Lord Jesus Christ, the Master
Designer of marriage, in a most intimate way—as your
Companion and Partner in life.

A Word from Pastor Raul

Marriage was designed by God. He intended for two people to be joined together—inseparable. Other than our relationship with God, marriage is the greatest relationship in the Christian life. I have been married to my wife Sharon for fifty years—that is a long time! Our marriage, at times, has been tough, but what has kept our marriage unbreakable? We made a vow—a covenant with each other—we would never divorce. Even as a nonbeliever, I knew I would not divorce my wife; our marriage was to be a permanent union, *until death do us part.*

During difficult times, we thought of our children; we knew it was vital for them that we follow God's model for marriage and for our grandchildren, as well.

Before I came to Christ, as a nonbeliever, I had a bad marriage. I was an abusive husband. When I came to Christ, I looked back in sadness at what I had done to Sharon; but because I truly repented, God forgave me. My wife also forgave me. Understandably, it took time for Sharon to rebuild her trust in me, but together we have moved forward in Christ.

Honestly, even as a pastor, I am not perfect, but I know that Sharon and I have remained together all these years, only by the grace of God. We have learned to get along together. In fact, my wife has been a real help to me in the ministry. She has stood by me in the call God has placed on my life. I have learned a lot from her because she grew up in ministry with her parents, who were missionaries in South America. Honestly, I do not think I would have made it in life without her by my side.

The marriage vow is an intimate, permanent bond that is made between a husband and his wife, before God. In the very beginning, God ordained marriage; He brought Adam and Eve together (Genesis 2:21–25).

Knowing marriage was ordained and arranged by the Lord, we can be sure it is the will of God for men and women to be joined together—to become one flesh.

Marriage is a blessed union between one man and one woman. Marriage is not something imperfect, created by man. One thing we must keep in mind: when God brings a man and woman together in marriage, it is a holy union. The man and woman are not perfect, but imperfect. When a couple submits to the Lord and to one another in love, their marriage will be blessed and fruitful.

If you had a troubled marriage before you came to the Lord, you can still have a marriage blessed by God, if you and your spouse both submit to the Lord and follow God's wisdom for your marriage, found in His Word.

To those who are going through a difficult period in your marriage, open your heart to God. Ask God to help you work on your marriage. He is the One who instituted marriage, so keep Him at the center, and you will have an inseparable union.

I am praying that through the power of the Holy Spirit, many marriages will be healed, as mine needed to be. As a pastor, I hope that husbands will have a renewed desire to love their wives, and the wives will unconditionally love their husbands. My wife and I are praying together that the Lord will do a tremendous work and use this book to help so many married couples in the church, and all around the world.

Souls for Christ,

Raul Ries

CHAPTER 1

THE MARRIAGE VOW

For wherever you go, I will go; and wherever you lodge, I will lodge; your people shall be my people, and your God, my God.

RUTH 1:16

I knew in my heart, Sharon was the woman I wanted to marry—I loved her. I stood at the altar, as the wedding ceremony began, with friends and family looking on. My mind drifted, *Here I have this beautiful woman who wants to marry me, a woman who wants to be my wife.* Finally, we reached the part in the ceremony where we exchanged our vows. Honestly, I had never heard the marriage vows before.

The ceremony did not make me feel nervous—I was just going through the motions to get married. I listened and repeated the vows but gave no real attention to what they meant. I never thought about them, and, at the time, I did not realize the importance of saying marriage vows. I was oblivious.

Although I had gone to church with Sharon, prayed at the altar, and even taken communion, I was not a Christian. In fact, I was responsible for getting her pregnant. The duty to do what was right was deeply rooted within me. I had taken responsibility, and as I stood at the altar, I thought over my obligation to find a good job to provide for my wife and child. I understood that I was not only becoming a husband but a father, as well.

My mind was not on the vows, but completely on Sharon. She looked beautiful, and seriously, my thoughts were on the wedding night!

As a Christian, Sharon was the one who knew the solemnity of taking vows before God, and she took them seriously. Years later, reflecting back on the moment she said her marriage vows, she wrote in her book, *My Husband My Maker*, not only her thoughts, but the spontaneous vow uttered from her heart to the Lord from the book of Ruth:

. . . I could see Raul clearly. His eyes were seeking mine. He was more splendid than all the princes in every storybook I had ever read. He was the fulfillment of every desire I had ever had. I was his bride, and he was my groom forever.

Radiant with confidence, he stood and waited, so very unaware of what he was getting into. The first two rows of seats, right in front of him, contained my priesthood family. I knew they would be praying, that day and every day that followed.

"Who gives this woman to be married to this man?" I heard the voice of my sweet Pastor, Carl Green. Then, together with my dad, they married us. Daddy gave me away and then moved to the altar to say the marriage vows with us.

I was vaguely troubled to see that Raul was paying very little attention to the ceremony. Instead, he spent those sacred minutes whispering to me, telling me how beautiful I looked. During the ring exchange, under his breath, I even heard him compliment my nails!

Despite his lack of interest, I managed to seriously and devotedly struggle through the vows. Raul's distractions invoked an unexpected urging deep within my being. I found myself saying my vows to Jesus, rather than to Raul. "Wherever You go, I will go;" I whispered to the Lord, "and wherever You lodge, I will lodge. Your people shall be my people, and [You] God shall be my God . . . I promise to love, cherish and obey You."

All at once, I could scarcely repeat the words. I became enveloped in a warmth that started from the top of my head and wrapped itself lovingly around me. It was a sensation unlike any I had ever experienced.

"I present to you Mr. and Mrs. Raul Andrew Ries." Pastor Green ended the ceremony by introducing us to the congregation. As we walked down the aisle, a soft Voice I had never heard before whispered to my heart, *I will never leave you.*

I don't know how, but I recognized the Captain's [Jesus'] voice. I had the unexpected perception I was glowing. I felt virgin and pure. I knew I was forgiven.

No matter what lay ahead, my future would always be warmed by God's presence. I would never leave Him, and He would never leave me—for better or for worse.

My Husband My Maker
Sharon Ries

A few years later, I accepted the Lord, and now, with my wife and two young boys, Raul and Shane, (Ryan was not born yet), peacefully relaxing at home, Sharon's parents, Ed and Naomi, who had been missionaries in Colombia and Chile for over twenty years, along with Pastor Daniel Cubillos, came knocking at the door.

Ed and Naomi introduced Pastor Daniel to me. He had attended their first Bible School in Chile in the early 1950s and had gone on to work with them planting churches. Daniel and his wife Maria had also been missionaries in Paraguay, Argentina and Bolivia, spending three years in each country.

Pastor Daniel eagerly wanted to know more about the Calvary Chapel Movement in the 70s—a Jesus Movement that I was zealously involved in with Pastor Chuck Smith. Pastor Daniel had a great interest in serving in ministry with us. Several young converts in his ministry in Valparaiso, Chile were involved in the Jesus Movement, which was spreading like wildfire among the hippies and drug culture on the extensive, sandy beaches.

Upon Pastor Daniel's return to Chile, he established a Calvary Chapel and worked with us for ten years, encouraging many young men to go out and start ministries which are still flourishing today. Throughout the years, he reached 22 countries with the Gospel of the Lord Jesus Christ. He was an amazing man who made a powerful impact on my life.

During Pastor Daniel's visit, I was moved by the Lord to restate my marriage vows to Sharon. How incredible it was for me to have this godly man be a part of this special moment in my life. As I thought back to the day of our wedding ceremony, when I said my vows to Sharon, I had not known what I was doing; but this time it would be different, because I now knew the seriousness of declaring a vow before God. In the Bible, a vow[1] before God is irrevocable, and obedience to God, for

---

[1] vow Hebrew *nadar* to promise: to do or give something to God; a promise to God. Greek *euche*: a wish; expressed as a petition to God: or in votive obligation; a prayer; a vow.

me, was more important than anything in the world. I believe in my heart that you have to keep your promises before God—to steadfastly worship Him in spirit and in truth.

Instantaneously, and without hesitation, I grabbed hold of our huge, black, family Bible with the words "Holy Bible" imprinted on the front cover in large gold letters. I had bought the Bible as a new believer and kept it on our living room coffee table. As we got on our knees, determinedly, I took Sharon's right hand, placed it on the Bible, and resolutely placed my own hand on top of hers. Slowly, I repeated the vows Pastor Daniel said in Spanish, every solemn word: "Do you testify before God that you will love her in health, sickness, and abundance or poverty?"

"Yes, I promise."

"Do you promise to respect her in the fear of the Lord, taking care of her every moment?"

"Yes, I promise."

"Do you promise to be faithful forgetting all other women, and living only for her until death separates you?"

"Yes, I promise."

"I declare you to be man and wife in the name of the Father, Son and Holy Spirit."

As I had spoken my vows before my wife and before God, I sincerely meant every word. I said my vows before God who I knew personally—the God I now feared and reverenced—and my God honored it.

After the vows were completed, my hand still on the family Bible, Pastor Daniel Cubillos also anointed me for service. This was a divine appointment in more ways than one. He was a man with a passion for God, who served the Lord until the end of his life.

WITH THIS RING

Looking back on this particular day when I said my marriage vows to love my wife, now knowing what they meant before God still makes me grin today. Imagine Sharon with her hair permed—frizzed out to the sky—wearing torn, blue, bell bottom jeans. Honestly, I was also dressed like a hippie but in zealousness of my conversion to Christ, I wore a big fish pendant that dangled loosely around my neck—a Christian symbol. In the earliest days of Christianity, the sign of the fish was used as a secret sign drawn in the sand by persecuted Christians.

My wife and I still have the same rings we chose for our wedding day, wide, gold bands—simple—very 70s. In a Christian wedding, when a couple says their vows to each other, the exchange of rings has great significance.

Marriage is sealed by the Holy Spirit. The rings symbolize God's everlasting love. It is a witness to people that you have made a commitment—a vow with your spouse. The ring itself is a circle, traditionally it speaks of *oneness*; the two individuals are becoming *one* in Christ. The confined center space of the ring symbolizes the exclusive relationship between a husband and wife in their marriage; the union is solely between a husband and wife—period. The outside of the ring is symbolic of the couples loved ones, family and friends.

Although it is good to receive godly advice from friends or from those within our families, they should never get involved in our personal marriage problems. Now as a husband and wife, when difficulties arise in your marriage, you both should go to the Lord. As much as possible, prayerfully keep situations between you and your spouse alone, and God will honor you both!

A SOLEMN PROMISE

When a man and woman get married, whether in the church or out of the church, they are nonetheless exchanging their vows before the Lord. He is present whether He is invited or not.

The *Merriam-Webster Dictionary* defines a *vow* as "a solemn promise," by which a person is bound to an act. When you say your marriage vows, you are making a solemn promise to your spouse and to the Lord. You are promising to love and honor your spouse throughout your entire life. People in the world, those who do not know Christ, will not understand the seriousness of declaring vows before God—they have no fear or reverence for God.

As Christians, God, in His Word has given us important precepts for making vows. God taught His people that if they made a vow to give to Him a sacrifice or offering, they should pay it:

> *"When you make a vow to the LORD your God, you shall not delay to pay it; for the LORD your God will surely require it of you, and it would be sin to you . . . That which has gone from your lips you shall keep and perform, for you voluntarily vowed to the LORD your God what you have promised with your mouth."*
>
> DEUTERONOMY 23:21, 23

When we voluntarily say our marriage vows before God, they are to be kept. Notice what God said; when we make a vow, we do it voluntarily. We are not forced to do it. We are not forced to marry each other. Our marriage vows are said before the Lord, and what we have promised before Him with our mouths, we must honor with our actions. Moses spoke a command from the Lord to the heads of the tribes of Israel saying:

> *"This is the thing which the LORD has commanded: If a man makes a vow to the LORD, or swears an oath to bind himself*

by some agreement, he shall not break his word; he shall do
according to all that proceeds out of his mouth."

NUMBERS 30:1–2

King David also knew the solemn responsibility of keeping his vows to God: *Vows made to You are binding upon me, O God* (Psalm 56:12).

WHEREVER YOU GO, I WILL GO

In the book of Ruth, Elimelech and his family traveled to Moab to escape a famine in the land of Israel. As they dwelt in this foreign land, tragedy struck. Naomi's husband Elimelech died, and after another ten years, her sons, Mahlon and Chilion, also died. Naomi, as a widow, had no means of providing for herself. Hearing that the Lord had visited her people in Israel with bread, she planned to return to her home in Bethlehem.

Naomi greatly discouraged her daughters-in-law, Orpah and Ruth, from following her. She told the young women, who were both Moabites, to go back to their families, because she had nothing to offer them—they had no future with her. Naomi had no more sons for them to marry, so she believed they would have a better life with their own people. Orpah desired to go with Naomi, but finally did what Naomi told her to do. She returned to Moab.

However, Ruth was determined to go with Naomi. She honored her dead husband's mother and clung to her. Ruth, despite an uncertain future, would return to Israel with Naomi. Ruth faithfully promised never to leave Naomi's side. She spoke a solemn vow of commitment to Naomi:

> *"Entreat me not to leave you, or to turn back from following*
> *after you; for wherever you go, I will go; and wherever you*
> *lodge, I will lodge; your people shall be my people, and your*

God, my God. Where you die, I will die, and there will I be buried. The LORD do so to me, and more also, if anything but death parts you and me."

RUTH 1:16–17

This vow is used in Christian marriage ceremonies today and is the vow my wife Sharon made to the Lord at our wedding. Notice how perfect these words are for making a solemn promise before the Lord to your spouse. These words completely reflect God's intentions for marriage. A husband and wife will surely be blessed by the Lord if they keep vows such as these, because they are making a promise to be true to one another. As they commit to be faithful to one another in their marriage, they will be able to endure difficult times and encourage one another to stay together. They will remain true to the marriage vow until the Lord takes them home—to heaven.

In the Bible, there are many married couples, but I want us to take a closer look at one couple who remained faithful to God and one another. Although God had a tremendous blessing for them, they would encounter many challenges. He would guide them, even in the midst of great trials.

BETROTHED

Mary and Joseph were ordinary people with humble backgrounds, yet God brought them together for an extraordinary purpose—to be the earthly parents to the Son of God.

Betrothed, they entered a time of engagement which typically lasted a year. Probably when they were young, a promise or contract had been made between their parents for a future marriage. The betrothal period was binding. Mary and Joseph would have been regarded as married during this period, and in such a permanent union, if they broke off their engagement, they would have to divorce.

While they were betrothed, and before they came together intimately, as prophesied in the Old Testament, the Holy Spirit overshadowed Mary, and she became pregnant with Jesus, the Son of God: *Therefore the LORD Himself will give you a sign: Behold, the virgin shall conceive and bear a Son, and shall call His name Immanuel* [God with us] (Isaiah 7:14).

Not fully understanding the miracle, and knowing that the Baby was not his, Joseph wanted to put her away—divorce her. However, he did not want any disgrace or harm to come to Mary, so he planned to leave her quietly:

> *Now the birth of Jesus Christ was as follows: After His mother Mary was betrothed to Joseph, before they came together, she was found with child of the Holy Spirit. Then Joseph her husband, being a just man, and not wanting to make her a public example, was minded to put her away secretly.*
>
> MATTHEW 1:18–19

Biblically, Joseph could break his vows because it appeared Mary had been unfaithful to him. The situation looked serious, and according to the Law, he had every right to break his vow to marry her and leave because of the circumstances. Mary was pregnant with someone else's child. Without the Lord's divine intervention, Joseph would have gone ahead and left Mary.

God knew Joseph was a just man and would have had a hard time accepting Mary's pregnancy, so He sent an angel to explain how this miracle happened and revealed to Joseph His purpose and plan for the Child:

> *But while he thought about these things, behold, an angel of the Lord appeared to him in a dream, saying, "Joseph, son of David, do not be afraid to take to you Mary your wife, for that which is conceived in her is of the Holy Spirit. And she will bring forth a Son, and you shall call His name Jesus, for He will save His people from their sins."*
>
> MATTHEW 1:20–21

Joseph was a godly man, and even though he could not fully comprehend what was happening, he trusted in the Lord. He was faithful to God and obedient to His call to be a husband. Placing his faith in God, he kept his vow to Mary and accepted her Child Jesus as his own:

> *Then Joseph, being aroused from sleep, did as the angel of the Lord commanded him and took to him his wife, and did not know her till she had brought forth her firstborn Son.*
>
> MATTHEW 1:24–25

God had ordained Mary and Joseph to be together, so He sent Joseph an angel with a message. Joseph could have doubted the angelic messenger, put Mary away, and moved on with his life. Joseph chose to believe God's promise and kept the vow he had made to Mary before God.

Unforeseen and difficult circumstances can happen in every marriage. Not being able to deal with the trials they face, one or the other spouse may decide it is time to leave. However, if a couple is walking with the Lord, trusting Him, and being faithful to the call of marriage, they will not break their vows. Instead, when the storms come, they will cling together as they hold on to the Lord and His promises.

CHAPTER 2

THE ORIGIN OF MARRIAGE

Therefore a man shall leave his father and mother and be joined to his wife, and they shall become one flesh.

GENESIS 2:24

Throughout the ages, marriage has suffered constant attack. It is thought to be a thing of the past, a religious tradition, and it is, in reality, becoming obsolete. Where did marriage originate? It originated in the heart of God. For Christians, the answer is clear and can be found in the Word of God. In Genesis, the first book of the Bible, we read how God, in the Garden of Eden, ordained the first marriage.

The LORD God made the man and the woman, and He brought them together: *Then the rib which the LORD God had taken from man He made into a woman, and He brought her to the man* (Genesis 2:22). Marriage was ordained in the book of Genesis during creation before Moses wrote the Law—the Ten Commandments—in the book of Exodus, as given to him by the LORD.

GOD'S PLAN FOR MARRIAGE

God, in Genesis 2, established the heavens and the earth and created all living creatures. After God created man and put him in the Garden of Eden, He saw Adam's loneliness and incompleteness: *And the LORD*

God said, "It is not good that man should be alone; I will make him a helper comparable[2] to him" (Genesis 2:18).

God made all the animals, yet they were not equal to Adam. He was to have dominion over them: *So, Adam gave names to all cattle, to the birds of the air, and to every beast of the field. But for Adam there was not found a helper comparable to him* (Genesis 2:20).

The most beautiful thing I saw from this verse was God's heart for Adam. Imagine Adam in the Garden of Eden after God created such uniquely designed animals, and yet Adam was lonely. The animals were not comparable to him, so God was going to create a companion for him.

At this time, woman had not been created, so Adam did not know his need for her, but God never intended for man to be alone. He knew of the emptiness and loneliness in his heart. He knew Adam needed someone like him. Adam needed a wife—a woman to fulfill his need for companionship.

Adam was content in the LORD, busy doing what God had called him to do, but God, knowing his need, put Adam to sleep. Remember, man was made from the ground—dirt: *And the LORD God formed man of the dust of the ground, and breathed into his nostrils the breath of life; and man became a living being* (Genesis 2:7), but woman would come from the man. When God made a companion for Adam, He made someone who was comparable, not an exact copy of him. He created a woman for man:

> *And the LORD God caused a deep sleep to fall on Adam, and he slept; and He took one of his ribs, and closed up the flesh in its*

---

[2]comparable Hebrew *ezer* aid: meaning help.

> *place. Then the rib which the Lord God had taken from man*
> *He made into a woman, and He brought her to the man.*
>
> GENESIS 2:21–22

Imagine, after looking at the monkeys and giraffes, Adam looked at woman. She must have been beautiful, and he must have thought and known she was created for just him! A wedding happened in the holiness and presence of God.

God is the Creator. Adam and Eve were both privileged to be created in God's image, but He differentiated between them. He made male and female. God established and ordained marriage between one man and one woman.

God made a woman to be the companion to Adam. The Lord God gave to Adam a woman who would help him in life. He created Eve to come alongside Adam and help him—to be a *help meet*. God gave him a gift. He intended for man to have a wife, and for man to worship God. It is important to know, God is the beginning of all things—He is the One who originated marriage.

It is really amazing how God took woman out of man. God took one of Adam's ribs and created woman from it. The word *rib* in the original Hebrew text means "curve-side." Notice, God did not take the woman from the bottom of man's feet, to be stepped on. He did not create her from the top of his head, so she could lord over him. He created the woman from the closest part to his heart, to stand by his side and be his companion, comparable to him.

God's decision to take the woman from the part closest to Adam's heart demonstrates His great care for women. He did not make her inferior to man, but equal to him. It is really important for us to understand God's order, because it is not man's order.

Many husbands dominate their wives, and there are wives who want to dominate their husbands. Neither is in agreement with biblical teaching. In order to have a blessed union, it is very important for a husband and wife to understand the biblical order God has given to them. God wants to work in every marriage through the power of the Holy Spirit, so that both husband and wife can accept what God has established in His Word as the foundation for their marriage.

It is really important to know that Adam and Eve had a perfect marriage because they were created in a perfect condition—physically and spiritually. They enjoyed the marriage relationship that God had ordained for them. They were in God's perfect will, walking with God in the Garden of Eden.

BONE OF MY BONES, FLESH OF MY FLESH

Adam was very pleased when God brought the woman to him. God had not disappointed Adam; He gave him exactly what was perfect for him—a companion and helper comparable to him. Adam named her *woman*:

> *And Adam said: "This is now bone of my bones and flesh of my flesh; she shall be called Woman, because she was taken out of Man." Therefore a man shall leave his father and mother and be joined to his wife, and they shall become one flesh.*
>
> GENESIS 2:23–24

This is it! God's perfect ordination of marriage concluded with these words: *Therefore a man shall leave his father and mother and be joined to his wife, and they shall become one flesh.* At this point in creation, God had only created Adam and Eve; neither of them had a father or a mother. God gave this instruction for those who would marry in the future. From this point forward, a man would leave his father and mother and become one flesh with his wife. The actual text in the King James Bible is this:

Therefore shall a man leave his father and his mother, and shall cleave[3] *unto his wife: and they shall be one flesh* (Genesis 2:24, KJV).

When a husband and wife come together in marriage, they become joined together in an inseparable bond. When a man and woman become one with each other, they do not forsake their fathers and mothers—they continue to have a loving and honorable relationship as God commanded: *"Honor your father and your mother, that your days may be long upon the land which the LORD your God is giving you"* (Exodus 20:12).

As a couple, they are to establish their own God-centered family. They are no longer joined to their father or mother; they are joined to each other. They are to build their lives together—biblically—grounded on God's Word.

At the end of Genesis 2, the creation of man was complete. There was perfect order in the Garden of Eden. The Scripture states: *And they were both naked, the man and his wife, and were not ashamed* (Genesis 2:25). God had brought Adam and Eve together—perfect and innocent—there was no sin. Everything was the way God had planned.

SATAN'S DECEPTION

In Genesis 3, Adam and Eve had a perfect marriage until sin entered in the Garden of Eden. It is important to understand, when God created Mankind, he gave them, the man and the woman, a free will. Remember, after creation, God had commanded Adam:

---

[3]cleave Hebrew *dabaq* impinge: to cling, adhere, catch by pursuit, abide fast, follow close, overtake, pursue hard, stick, take or to be joined together.

"Of every tree of the garden you may freely eat; but of the tree of the knowledge of good and evil you shall not eat, for in the day that you eat of it you shall surely die."[4]

GENESIS 2:16–17

In the Garden of Eden, Satan saw an opportunity to speak with Eve and deceive her. Satan was deceptive; he knew precisely when to make his move. Satan, as a lion on the prowl, looked for a victim, and the victim he found was the woman—Eve—the weaker vessel.

In the Garden of Eden, Satan used the serpent, a beautiful creature of God, to speak to the woman. It is believed the serpent stood upright until after the fall of man, when God cursed the serpent, limiting the creature to crawl on the ground (Genesis 3:14). In Revelation 12 Satan is referred to as the Dragon. The Greek word for *Dragon* is "serpent." Also, Satan transforms himself into an angel of light. Interestingly, in Isaiah 14:12 Satan is called Lucifer, which in Hebrew language literally means "the shining one."

GOD'S WORD CHALLENGED

Satan will always attack the deity of Christ, the Word of God, and the work of the Holy Spirit. How did Satan deceive the woman? The first thing Satan did was to challenge the Word of God. He brought doubt into the mind of the woman. In Genesis 3:1, Satan began to play with Eve's mind, saying: *"Has God indeed said, 'You shall not eat of every tree of the garden?'"* Notice Eve's reply as she answered Satan:

"We may eat the fruit of the trees of the garden; but of the fruit

---

[4]die: Mankind was created to live forever in holy communion with God. Adam was warned by God not to eat of the tree of the knowledge of good and evil, otherwise he would suffer death, in his physical body and spiritual being.

*of the tree which is in the midst of the garden, God has said,
'You shall not eat it, nor shall you touch it, lest you die.'"*

GENESIS 3:2–3

At first, Eve began her answer by quoting God's Word correctly. She spoke truth, but then she added to God's Word: *nor shall you touch it . . .* and she softened God's command in saying *lest you die,* when God had strongly warned *you shall surely die.* Then Satan subtlety contradicted God's Word and blatantly lied to her: "*For God doth know that in the day ye eat thereof, then your eyes shall be opened, and ye shall be as gods,*[5] *knowing good and evil*" (Genesis 3:5, KJV).

Satan defamed God's character and tempted Eve. He told her she would become like God, but God never said that. There is only one God! Satan was lying to her. Yes, Eve would know good and evil, but why? Satan knew that if she sinned, she would acquire knowledge. The word *knowing* literally means, "the practical ability to know what is right from wrong." It was knowledge which was unknown to them, and only known to God.

By engaging in a conversation that was in direct rebellion against God's Word, Eve was deceived by the serpent—Satan. She disobeyed God, she ate the forbidden fruit, and she sinned against God. Eve also gave her husband Adam to eat fruit from the tree of the knowledge of good and evil:

So when the woman saw that the tree was good for food, that it was pleasant to the eyes, and a tree desirable to make one wise, she took of its fruit and ate. She also gave to her husband with her, and he ate.

GENESIS 3:6

---

[5] gods Hebrew *elohim* gods: in the ordinary sense; can be applied to magistrates; angels or judges—mighty ones.

Notice the act of violating God's Word in the three areas of temptation; she *saw* that the fruit was *pleasant to the eyes,* so she coveted it. The fruit was *desirable* to make her wise—*the pride of life.* She *ate* the fruit, which appealed to the *lust of her flesh.* Eve's lust of the eyes, pride of life, and lust of the flesh caused her to give in to Satan's temptations, causing her to disobey God and yield to sin. Eve then gave the forbidden fruit to Adam, and he ate. Both of them willfully fell into sin—this was the fall of man.[6]

The instant they sinned, they died spiritually, and their eyes were opened[7]—they had an awareness of their sin. For the first time, Adam and Eve knew they had fallen and lost their purity. They were naked and, consequently, they experienced shame: *Then the eyes of both of them were opened, and they knew that they were* naked; and they sewed fig leaves together and made *themselves coverings* (Genesis 3:7).

Beforehand, Adam and Eve could not see their nakedness; their eyes were only opened to see God and His creation in the Garden of Eden—paradise. They were righteous people who were in the presence of God, perfect—without sin. When Adam and Eve sinned against God, from that very moment, they became imperfect—falling from a state of innocent obedience to God, to a state of disobedience to Him.

This was the beginning of man's first consciousness of guilt. In shame, they sought to cover their nakedness with fig leaves[8] when they needed to be covered in God's righteousness.

---

[6]fall of man: "the fall," is a term used in Christianity to describe the transition of the first man and woman from a state of innocent obedience to God to a state of guilty disobedience.

[7]opened Hebrew *paqach* to open: the senses, especially the eyes; to be observant; to enable to see things which otherwise are hidden from the eyes of mortals.

[8]fig leaves: perishable coverings; Adam's and Eve's fruitless efforts to cover themselves for their guilty souls.

MARRIAGE RESTORED

In Genesis 3:8–9, as Adam and Eve hid in shame, they may have heard the voice of God in a much different tone:

> *And they heard the sound of the* Lord *God walking in the garden in the cool of the day, and Adam and his wife hid themselves from the presence of the* Lord *God among the trees of the garden. Then the* Lord *God called to Adam and said to him, "Where are you?"*

Adam and Eve, instead of fellowshipping with God as they had in times past, sought to hide from the presence of God. Sin had separated them from God and caused them to hide from Him. They had fallen from the true perfect state they had been created in, to the natural man—being ruled by their carnal desires—they were spiritually dead. The Lord knew they had fallen from the spiritual realm.

Notice that God addressed Adam first, showing the man's created position of headship. Paul affirms Adam's authority when he taught on the role of a woman regarding teaching and having authority over man: *And I do not permit a woman to teach or to have authority over a man . . . For Adam was formed first, then Eve. And Adam was not deceived, but the woman being deceived, fell into transgression* (1 Timothy 2:12–14).

God knew where Adam and Eve were hiding—He is omniscient, knowing all things. The Lord called to Adam with words of compassion and love, looking for Him to repent.

Adam knew God's voice, but experienced a new human emotion—fear—when he spoke with the Lord: *". . . I heard Your voice in the garden, and I was afraid because I was naked; and I hid myself"* (Genesis 3:10).

In Genesis 3:11, God looked for an honest confession from Adam concerning his sin: *"Who told you that you were naked? Have you eaten from the tree of which I commanded you that you should not eat?"* God wanted to know, *"Did you disobey Me, Adam?"*

Instead of fully repenting of his disobedience to God, Adam not only blamed his wife, but also blamed God for giving him the woman and he made an excuse: *"The woman whom You gave to be with me, she gave me of the tree, and I ate"* (Genesis 3:12). The woman did it! Knowing God is omniscient, he confessed that he was naked, afraid, and he hid himself from God's presence. Adam confessed he had eaten from the forbidden fruit!

When a man or a woman chooses to disobey God, it brings distrust, betrayal and division into their loving marital union. Imagine the damage sin did to the first marriage relationship that ever existed! They sinned against God and betrayed each other.

God then asked the woman about her actions: *"What is this you have done?"* The woman said, *"The serpent deceived me, and I ate"* (Genesis 3:13). Eve, not acknowledging any fear like Adam did, also made an excuse for her disobedience to God and blamed the serpent.

After God received the man's and his wife's excuses, He did not judge them first; He immediately judged the serpent—Satan:

> *"Because you have done this, you are cursed more than all cattle, and more than every beast of the field; on your belly you shall go, and you shall eat dust all the days of your life."*
>
> GENESIS 3:14

Notice, in the middle of God's judgment, He pronounced the great promise of the Redeemer coming to defeat Satan: *"And I will put enmity between you and the woman, and between your seed and her Seed; He shall bruise your head, and you shall bruise His heel"* (Genesis 3:15).

Here is the first prophecy in the Bible about the future virgin birth of Jesus Christ—the Seed. The serpent had deceived the woman, but the Savior of mankind would come through the womb of a woman. I love that! God would take care of man's sin by sending His Only Begotten Son, Jesus Christ, and Satan would be defeated.

God spoke His judgment to the woman: *"I will greatly multiply your sorrow and your conception; in pain you shall bring forth children; your desire shall be for your husband, and he shall rule over you"* (Genesis 3:16).

It was not like that in the beginning in the Garden of Eden. In Genesis 1:26–28, both the man and the woman were made in the image of God. They were to be fruitful, multiply, replenish the earth, subdue it, and have dominion over every living thing. The woman, because of the curse, would now conceive in sorrow and bring forth her children in pain. She would have a longing desire toward her husband, and he would rule over her.

Then God spoke His judgment to Adam:

> *Then to Adam He said, "Because you have heeded the voice of your wife, and have eaten from the tree of which I commanded you, saying, 'You shall not eat of it': "Cursed is the ground for your sake; in toil you shall eat of it all the days of your life. Both thorns and thistles it shall bring forth for you, and you shall eat the herb of the field. In the sweat of your face you shall eat bread till you return to the ground, for out of it you were taken; for dust you are, and to dust you shall return."*
>
> GENESIS 3:17–19

The book of Genesis gave us the key to salvation. The ground being cursed, Adam would endure hard labor for the rest of his life. Thorns and thistles speak of the curse. Wearing a crown of thorns, Christ became a curse for us when He gave His life for mankind on the Cross (Galatians 3:13).

Adam then gave his wife a name: *And Adam called his wife's name Eve because she was the mother of all living* (Genesis 3:20), meaning "life or life-giver." Adam and Eve in their shame covered themselves with fig leaves, but God provided them coverings, not only for their nakedness, but to cover their sin: *Also for Adam and his wife the LORD God made tunics of skin, and clothed them* (Genesis 3:21).

In the beginning, God provided atonement[9] for mankind. To cover the man and woman with tunics of skins, there had to be the shedding of the blood of an animal. The shedding of blood would forever be symbolic of the sacrifice of Christ, the Lamb of God, for the forgiveness and purging of man's sin.

In the Old Testament, God required the blood of a goat, a lamb or turtle dove for a sin offering. This was only a covering for sin—the sin of man was put away, but not wiped away permanently. When Jesus gave His life for mankind and shed His blood on the Cross, sin was put away once and for all; man's sins were atoned for: *as far as the east is from the west, so far has He removed our transgressions from us* (Psalm 103:12). The penalty for Adam and Eve's sin was not only for them, but for all mankind—all the generations to come. We have been forgiven!

---

[9]atonement: propitiation, to cover, to cancel, to cleanse, forgive, purge away; make reconciliation to cover over; without an atoning sacrifice there is no access for sinful men to come into the presence of the Holy God.

The first married couple, because of their disobedience to God, was cast out of the protection of the Garden of Eden (Genesis 3:23–24). Sin had entered the world. Adam and Eve gave birth to Cain and Abel, and the first murder took place; Cain killed his brother Abel. Through God's love and mercy, *Adam knew His wife again, and she bore a son and named him Seth, "For God has appointed another seed for me instead of Abel, whom Cain killed"* (Genesis 4:25). Christ, the Promised One came through the lineage of their son Seth.

Adam and his wife Eve continued to conceive sons and daughters in their own likeness. Adam lived nine hundred years with the hope of the coming Savior that would come through the womb of the woman.

God's original plan for marriage was marred in the Garden of Eden because of Adam's and Eve's rebellion and disobedience. As we walk in obedience to the Word of God, if we sin, and repent, we are forgiven: *If we confess our sins, He is faithful and just to forgive us our sins and to cleanse us from all unrighteousness* (1 John 1:9), and we can enjoy the blessedness that God intended in the beginning for our marriages.

CHAPTER 3

SUBMISSION, LOVE AND INTIMACY

. . . submitting to one another in the fear of God.

EPHESIANS 5:21

In the second chapter, we established that marriage from the very beginning was ordained by God. In Genesis, He instituted marriage to be a partnership between the man and the woman. He made them comparable, but not exactly the same. He made them to complement one another, so they would be able to come alongside each other. They would be stronger together than separate.

From Genesis to Revelation, God gave laws, commands and instructions concerning the submission, love and intimacy that must exist between a man and a woman in marriage. Examples of marriages are portrayed throughout the Scriptures. Some of them failed because of man's absolute disobedience to God. Those that were successful adhered to God's instructions for marriage, despite their tendencies to disobey. If couples want long-lasting, intimate and fulfilling marriages, they need to know God's Word and live in obedience to it.

Many couples go into marriage completely unaware of how they are to behave toward each other. A relationship between a husband and a wife should be based upon biblical principles. The Bible teaches Christians, not nonbelievers, God's design for marriage.

For a strong marriage, both the husband and wife need to know and understand that God has designed an individual role for each one of them. What does the Bible teach a husband or wife about their place in the marriage? What different responsibilities must each spouse fulfill?

In the Word of God, no matter what Scriptures you read in regard to marriage, the Apostle Paul gave three main principles for couples to follow in their roles to unite them—submission, love and intimacy.

UNITED IN SUBMISSION

Paul addressed the relationship between a man and woman specifically in Ephesians 5:22–33, but before he did, he left the body of Christ with these profound words: . . . *submitting to one another in the fear of God* (Ephesians 5:21). All believers are to be in submission one to another—united in the fear of the Lord.

This word of wisdom is important in our Christian walk, and especially in our marriages. Paul's exhortation of submitting to one another leads right into the subject of husbands and wives.

Paul instructed wives in Ephesians 5:22, *submit to your own husbands, as to the Lord.* Then Paul exhorted husbands a few verses down in Ephesians 5:25, *love your wives.* Understand, if a husband loves his wife, she will naturally submit to her husband's leadership; otherwise, a good marriage becomes impossible.

However, I believe for many women the idea of submitting to their husbands is terrifying. The word *submit* can have a very negative connotation due to the suffering women have endured in abusive relationships.

A woman may think submission makes her weak, and she will become her husband's slave or doormat. Misuse of biblical submission is due to the lack of understanding of what God intended it to mean.

The Greek word Paul used in Ephesians 5:22 is *hupotussō*, and according to *Strong's Exhaustive Concordance*, it means "to arrange under." It was a Greek military term meaning "to arrange [troop divisions] in a military fashion under the command of a leader." As a nonmilitary use, it was "a voluntary attitude of giving in, cooperating, assuming responsibility, and carrying a burden."

Paul spoke about submission in the marriage like it is in the military. A soldier learns to submit to his commander, otherwise, he would not remain in the military. Think about it. In every capacity of our lives there is someone you are in submission to. Wherever you work or play, there is some type of authority over you. In your place of work, someone is in authority, and you need to be in submission to them, or it could be you have been placed in a position of authority over others. Ultimately, we all are to be in submission to the Lordship of Jesus Christ.

When we look at the proper intent of the word *submission* in a marriage relationship, it means a wife voluntarily chooses to cooperate with her husband. I like that. When a wife submits to her husband, she makes the decision to willingly assume responsibility and help carry life's burdens with her husband. A wife does not come against her husband but works with him for the best of their marriage and family. It is amazing how simple submitting is when a man and woman conduct their marriage in obedience to the Word of God.

Jesus Christ is the best example of submission given to us because He willingly submitted to the Father's plan of mankind's salvation. Jesus obediently surrendered to the death on the Cross, where He shed His blood to pay the penalty for our sins. Christ redeemed us and rescued us from an eternity separated from God. Seriously, there was nothing weak in His actions (Philippians 2:5–8).

God has not only established the chain of command in marriage, but also the authority—headship: *For the husband is head of the wife, as also Christ is head of the church; and He is the Savior of the body* (Ephesians 5:23). In the marriage relationship, the husband is to take a God-ordained leadership position. He is to be the *head of the wife*—become the spiritual leader.

Then Paul concluded the wives' responsibility by saying: *Therefore, just as the church is subject to Christ, so let the wives be to their own husbands in everything* (Ephesians 5:24). The word *everything* speaks of everything in the Lord—everything that is right. Marriage was designed to be a clear reflection of the relationship between Christ and the Church.

Therefore, God called the husband to be the head of the wife, just as Christ is the head of the Church. When wives submit to their husbands, they are actually in submission to the Lord. It is not always easy for wives to submit to their husbands, but in Christ, they can. If a husband is fully submitted to the Lord, a wife will trust her husband.

Paul once again clarified the wife's role in submitting to her husband in Colossians 3:18: *Wives, submit to your own husbands, as is fitting in the Lord.* Notice Paul's use of the word *fitting, which* means "right, proper, suitable, and appropriate." Men are not to take advantage of their wives' submission and be abusive. Understand, a wife should submit to only what is right in God's eyes. A wife should not submit to anything that is sinful before God.

SUBMISSION TO AN UNSAVED SPOUSE

Some wives today may ask, "How can I submit to a nonbeliever?" The Apostle Peter answers that very question. In 1 Peter 3:1–6, he spoke about submission in marriage and addressed the sometimes difficult environment when a woman is married to a nonbeliever.

Peter knew women needed guidance from the Holy Spirit because, in this culture, women were not looked up to. It was common, as it is today in many cultures, for a husband to have concubines—girlfriends for pleasure and a wife to take care of his children and other needs. This was a husband's mentality. Women had no freedoms; they were like slaves—mistreated.

Peter spoke to women who lived in a dark, pagan culture, being married himself (Luke 4:38–39); he gave good advice to wives on what to do. He instructed them on how they could win their husbands to the Lord by their manner of life:

> *Wives, likewise, be submissive to your own husbands, that even if some do not obey the word, they, without a word, may be won by the conduct of their wives, when they observe your chaste conduct accompanied by fear.*
>
> 1 PETER 3:1–2

Peter knew that God would work through a wife who was a fully committed Christian. She would be a godly influence and appeal to her husband through her submission and conduct. A wife's better quality of life and the way she was living would draw him to the Lord—not by preaching to him all the time. Wives, husbands are watching your life. Is it pure in conduct, accompanied by the fear of the Lord?

Humorously, I tell wives married to nonbelievers, when you make your husband's sandwiches, do not place little tracts in them, so when he eats, he sees and reads the message, "Thus says the Lord, you're going to hell!" Be careful not to turn your husband off and push him away from Christ!

Seriously, how can a nonbelieving husband come to the Lord? Through the wife's conduct and manner of life—the wife's behavior. If your husband is not a Christian, he could not care less about the Word of God. He certainly does not want to be preached at. Honestly, men hate nagging. The best thing to do is pray and be silent, as the Lord works on your husband's heart; then He will open the door for you to speak with him about your faith.

However, if you are a wife of a nonbeliever, and he is physically, verbally and emotionally abusive, there is a point in time when you can separate for your own safety and allow God time to work on your marriage.

As a nonbeliever, I did not want to be preached at—I did not want to hear about Christ. I watched Sharon; I saw Christ in her—it bugged me. I could see God in her life. Sharon was a praying wife; she was in the Word of God. As a mother, when our children were little, she would teach them Bible stories and pray with them.

I had no shame or feelings, especially after coming back from Vietnam and being locked up in a mental institution for six months—I did not care about anything. I would smack her, push her around, and even kick her, but she never retaliated. I remember one time, I was angry with Sharon because she was on her way to church, and I went off and kicked her—she had a baby in her arms. An angel must have protected her, because I should have broken her leg. That is how mean I was, but nothing happened to her.

Sharon continued to take care of our boys, loving them and teaching them to love their dad. I was cold and uncaring, yet she always told them, "You need to forgive and love your father." God saw what I did to her; He was there and the Lord eventually humbled me. As I watched Sharon live her life for Christ, the Holy Spirit pursued my life.

Yet I was consumed with anger; I was convinced she was going to take the children and leave me. I was not going to allow anyone to have my wife and our boys, even if I had to end, not only my life, but theirs. While Sharon was in church one day, in anger, I hit the television with the butt of my rifle. The television came on. A man was being interviewed about the Jesus movement by Kathryn Kuhlman, a well-known evangelist who was hosting healing crusades in the 1970s in the heart of Los Angeles, California.

The Holy Spirit spoke to me through the man I saw on television, who was sharing about God's unconditional love and forgiveness for sinners. I later learned the man was Pastor Chuck Smith. I got saved in the same house where I was abusing my wife. It was a miracle of God!

Today, my wife, three sons and I have a loving relationship with each other. It was because of my wife's faithfulness to the Lord that my children love me. They knew I was a rat, so it was not because of me. Looking back, my boys should hate me—I was so violent—but God is the One who did the work in my life.

If you are married to someone who has a hardened heart, God is the only One who can bring the change. I believe with all my heart, if you are Christian woman who is constantly talking to your husband about the Lord, but your behavior is rebellious, he is never going to get saved—no possible way. If you are yelling and screaming at your husband, he will rebel against you even more. Take him before the Lord in prayer. God can do a better job. It is real important that you pray!

Peter continued his advice to wives:

> *Do not let your adornment be merely outward—arranging the hair, wearing gold, or putting on fine apparel—rather let it be the hidden person of the heart, with the incorruptible*

beauty of a gentle and quiet spirit, which is very precious in the sight of God.

1 PETER 3:3–4

Underline this important verse in your Bible; it is a vital principle to remember. The best way for a wife to influence her husband is not through her outer appearance, but through the hidden person of the heart. Peter told women that true and lasting beauty was not in the way they put on their makeup, dresses or jewelry. The apostle placed the emphasis on a woman's inward beauty, the hidden person of the heart—having a meek and peaceful disposition. This means no nagging, no screaming or yelling—just being godly.

Remember, you are married to the Lord first. If you aim to please God, then you are going to please your husband. A wife should not bring attention to herself so men can lust after her—it is not pleasing to the Lord. However, a Christian woman should take care of her outer appearance, she should look beautiful outwardly and inwardly, but her main focus should be beautifying the hidden woman of the heart.

During the Jesus movement, women were going to church not wearing bras—it was a big problem. Chuck Smith knew, as women studied the Word of God, the Holy Spirit would speak to them to be dressed properly—modestly. Then women could become godly examples for their daughters.

Peter also encouraged women married to nonbelievers to trust the Lord. He directed them to the examples of godly women in the Old Testament. They were a model to follow in the way they dressed themselves and in their submissiveness to their own husbands. Peter mentioned Sarah as a model wife—though she had disobeyed God at times, she remained submissive and obedient to the Lord and her husband, Abraham:

> *For in this manner, in former times, the holy women who trusted in God also adorned themselves, being submissive to their own husbands, as Sarah obeyed Abraham, calling him lord, whose daughters you are if you do good and are not afraid with any terror.*
>
> 1 PETER 3:5–6

Sarah was not forced to be submissive to her husband—she loved Abraham, and she wanted to please the Lord. Sarah decided to honor her husband, so she called Abraham *lord*. She addressed him with a title of respect—it would be the same as using the title of respect *Sir* to a man in a position of authority today.

As a wife, you do not have to call your husband *lord*, but the Word of God instructs . . . *let the wife see that she respects her husband* (Ephesians 5:33). If you truly want God to work in your marriage, then re-read these passages on marriage, learn from godly women in the Bible, trust the Lord, and put your life in the hands of God.

UNITED IN LOVE

In Ephesians 5:25, Paul instructed husbands to love their wives: *Husbands, love your wives, just as Christ also loved the church and gave Himself for her.* A quote from a pastor and American theologian, RC Sproul, will help husbands to understand and further consider the seriousness of Paul's command to husbands: "Husbands, love your wives, is not a nugget of human wisdom—it is the mandate of Almighty God."

Notice the unconditional love a husband must have for his wife. It is not just a physical love. Paul said to love your wife as *Christ loved the church and gave Himself for her*. It is a sacrificial love. The husband is to give himself for his wife as Christ gave Himself for the Church.

Again, husbands have Christ's example to follow. In His great love for the Church, Christ gave up His life. If a husband loves his wife as Christ loves the Church, he is willing to deny himself and think first of his wife. First and foremost, a husband's responsibility in loving his wife is to lay a biblical foundation through the Word of God in their marriage. He must provide spiritual guidance and help her to grow closer to the Lord: *Husbands, love your wives, just as Christ also loved the church and gave Himself for her, that He* [Christ] *might sanctify and cleanse her* [the Church] *with the washing of water by the word* (Ephesians 5:25–26).

I am not telling husbands to do a four-hour Bible study with their wives, but as the spiritual leader, it is important to connect with each other regularly in a devotional time and pray together. Husbands, allow the Lord to give you wisdom in sharing with your wife, as you read and pray with her. Then you both will be spiritually prepared for the day.

It is important to understand that not all couples come together to read the Bible. My wife and I prefer to have our devotional time separately. I go upstairs, and my wife remains downstairs. Then, at times, we come together and share with each other what the Lord has shown to us. Whatever works in your marriage is great—just make sure you are both in God's Word.

The worst thing to happen in a marriage is when a husband, as the head of the house, does not know God's Word. How can he give spiritual guidance to his wife? If the husband does not have a close relationship with the Lord, he cannot be the spiritual head of his home. When a husband fails to be the spiritual head of his home or refuses to lead, then a Christian woman must take that role, especially for the sake of her children.

When a husband neglects to be with his wife, leaving her alone, not praying with her or watching over her, the enemy—Satan—has a field day. He sees an opportunity to attack the wife—he knows she is more vulnerable. Without any spiritual leadership, the marriage will not be strong, and the family will be an easy target for Satan.

It is also important for the husbands to know that, in the end, they are the ones who will present their wives to the Lord, just as Christ presents His Church to Himself: . . . *that He* [Christ] *might present her to Himself a glorious church, not having spot or wrinkle or any such thing, but that she should be holy and without blemish* (Ephesians 5:27).

Imagine husbands who have abused their wives and not repented. How will they be able to stand before the Lord, presenting their wives before Him, emotionally beaten and physically battered? Husbands must treat their wives with great love and great kindness.

Paul went even further in his description of the love a man must have for his wife. He must love her as much as he loves his own body:

> *So husbands ought to love their own wives as their own bodies; he who loves his wife loves himself. For no one ever hated his own flesh, but nourishes and cherishes it, just as the Lord does the church.*
>
> EPHESIANS 5:28–29

Paul, in his exhortation, told husbands to nourish and cherish their wives. He was speaking of emotional support. Husbands need to learn how to give of themselves, to be understanding and compassionate. Men love themselves, take care of themselves, and think about themselves all the time. God knows men have a real big problem with their egos.

In the gym, you always see men loving their bodies, pumping up their muscles, working out, the whole thing, and looking in the mirror more than anyone else—they are number one. I can tell you this, because I am a man. When I am hungry, I get food. When I am tired, I sleep. I do not wait for someone to take care of me. I make sure my needs are met.

As husbands, do we spend the same amount of time and effort in loving our wives? Christ demonstrated His love toward the Church throughout His life, and when He gave His life on the Cross. This is the sacrificial love we must have for our wives.

PROVIDING FOR YOUR FAMILY

A God-ordained way to demonstrate Christ's love to your wife is to provide for her needs. Paul explained the seriousness of a man's role in providing for his wife and family to Timothy, a young minister: *But if anyone does not provide for his own, and especially for those of his household, he has denied the faith and is worse than an unbeliever* (1 Timothy 5:8).

A husband should be working and supplying the needs of the home financially. God called the man to be the provider of his home, not the woman. The Word of God teaches the privilege a woman has been given in being a keeper of the home and raising a godly heritage (Proverbs 31).

During tough financial times, a wife may have to go to work. However, there are men who send their wives out to work when it is not necessary. I know there are lazy men who do not want to work, but there are many more who want to work and build a future for their families—amazing! They are good stewards, maintaining their homes and making sure there is enough money to provide food and clothing for their wives and children. Husbands and fathers have a great responsibility before God as the heads of their homes.

Paul in Ephesians 5 has a few more words for husbands and wives. As members of Christ's body, they each must reflect His selfless love: *For we are members of His body, of His flesh and of His bones* (Ephesians 5:30). Through Christ's love a couple can become joined together as one—inseparable. Ephesians 5:31 repeats Genesis 2:24, when God instituted marriage between Adam and Eve and all future generations: *"For this reason a man shall leave his father and mother and be joined to his wife, and the two shall become one flesh."*

There is no way a man and a woman can become one if they are striving to selfishly live their own lives. Without love, respect, and submission to one to another, the couple cannot become one with each other and in Christ, fulfilling their roles as God intended in the marriage, bringing peace.

THE MYSTERY OF MARITAL ONENESS

Paul, in a final exhortation regarding the marriage relationship, spoke to both the husband and the wife:

> *This is a great mystery, but I speak concerning Christ and the church. Nevertheless let each one of you in particular so love his own wife as himself, and let the wife see that she respects her husband.*
>
> EPHESIANS 5:32–33

It is amazing to me the way Christ protects and watches over His Church. Just as Christ desires what is best for His Bride and loves the Church, so a husband must love His wife, and a wife needs to respect her husband.

It is so beautiful when the Lord, through His Spirit, enables the husband to have a Christ-like love for his wife. He will genuinely love her like Christ loves the Church. When the husband knows God's Word and takes the role of the spiritual head of his home seriously, his wife will be able to respect and reverence her husband.

If the husband loves his wife, she will submit—she will not challenge him. A woman will challenge a husband's authority when he is not the spiritual authority in the home. A wife needs to be reassured of her husband's love. She will be comforted by knowing her husband has her best interest at heart. She will trust him with her heart and with her family. If a husband is truly committed to the Lord, she will feel secure in their marriage.

It seems to me men are more unfeeling and women are more emotional and sympathetic. As a husband, I do not need to be told constantly that I am loved. Sharon demonstrates her love to me by her actions—that is enough for me. She may tell me once in a while that she loves me. I appreciate it, that is nice, I am good. I know my wife loves me. God instructs man to love his wife! (Ephesians 5:25)

Marriage takes two people committed to living the crucified life— death to self. It is amazing when couples are willing to work together on their relationship to keep their mutual love growing. Their marriage will be blessed with comfort and peace.

Keep in mind, if you want to have marital oneness, you must work together to keep Christ at the center of your relationship.

UNITED IN INTIMACY

God ordained marriage so that a relationship between a man and woman would provide companionship, love and intimacy. God brought the man and woman together, and they were to become one, which happens in sexual intimacy. Once you are married, you are free to engage in sexual intimacy without any reservations, because the marriage bed is undefiled: *Marriage is honorable among all; and the bed undefiled; but fornicators and adulterers God will judge* (Hebrews 13:4).

Since we know God ordained marriage, the union between man and woman must be honored. God is clear in His Word regarding sexual intimacy in marriage. There is no room for another person to become intimate with either one of them outside of their marriage. Be aware, Satan will come along and bring adulterous temptations to cause a wedge to divide and destroy the marriage: . . . *an adulteress will prey upon his precious life. Can a man take fire to his bosom, and his clothes not be burned?* (Proverbs 6:26–27) Adultery will destroy the intimate bond between a man and a woman—period.

The couple must protect this intimate relationship that God has blessed them with by being faithful to each other in order to have a fulfilled sexual union:

> *Let your fountain be blessed, and rejoice with the wife of your youth. As a loving deer and a graceful doe, let her breasts satisfy you at all times; and always be enraptured with her love.*
>
> PROVERBS 5:18–19

REFRAINING FROM SEXUAL INTIMACY

The Apostle Paul gave advice to married couples who were having problems in their marriage relationship. He told them:

> *Let the husband render to his wife the affection due her, and likewise also the wife to her husband. The wife does not have authority over her own body, but the husband does. And likewise the husband does not have authority over his own body, but the wife does. Do not deprive one another except with consent for a time, that you may give yourselves to fasting and prayer; and come together again so that Satan does not tempt you because of your lack of self-control.*
>
> 1 CORINTHIANS 7:3–5

In agreement, a married couple can refrain from sexual intimacy. As they separate, the time apart is set aside for prayer and fasting. Then they are to come back together to avoid being tempted into adultery by Satan. It is very clear in the Scriptures. When there is no sexual intimacy, it creates a problem in the marriage, and adultery can happen.

There are different situations when a husband and a wife can no longer be intimate with each other. In that case they must exercise self-control through the power of the Holy Spirit (Galatians 5:22–23).

SEXUAL PERVERSION

There are women who come in for counseling who say their husbands have been drawn into pornography, and they want them to perform sexually the same way. A wife does not have to submit to sexual perversion. A woman is not an object to be exploited. Pornography is polluted—perversion. A married couple must be in agreement with each other on how they perform sexually with each other. God made sex beautiful for a husband and a wife to enjoy pleasure with each other. Scriptures record the sexual perversion that took place among the Canaanite, the Greek and the Roman societies. It is evident in the archeological history of these cultures, which is still displayed today in museums. Worldwide and in America, pornography is widespread, raking in billions of dollars.

God has a unique plan for every marriage, and His desire is to bless every husband and wife. At times, a couple can fall short of each other's expectations and can have serious problems in their relationship. We are not perfect, but if Christ is the center of our marriage, and we build on His foundation for marriage, I believe husbands and wives can work out any problem—fully and completely.

THE BLESSED GIFT OF CHILDREN

While intimacy is vital in a marriage, God also created it to bless a couple with children and to populate the earth. In Genesis 1:27–28, God told Adam and Eve to have children:

> *So God created man in His own image; in the image of God He created him; male and female He created them. Then God blessed them, and God said to them, "Be fruitful and multiply; fill the earth and subdue it . . . "*

It is beautiful to have a lot of children in the Lord. It is a blessing from the Lord. Think about it; if you bring them up knowing God, they will stand by you throughout your life:

> *Behold, children are a heritage from the LORD, the fruit of the womb is a reward. Like arrows in the hand of a warrior, so are the children of one's youth. Happy is the man who has his quiver full of them; they shall not be ashamed, but shall speak with their enemies in the gate.*
>
> PSALM 127:3–5

The Psalmist blesses the man who fears the Lord and walks in His ways:

> *Your wife shall be like a fruitful vine in the very heart of your house, your children like olive plants all around your table. Behold, thus shall the man be blessed who fears the LORD . . . Yes, may you see your children's children.*
>
> PSALM 128:3–4, 6

As you walk with God in the fear of the LORD, you will be a witness to your family, and you and your family will have a life blessed by the LORD. I enjoy my grandchildren; I am blessed by them. They are amazing! God has a plan for each one of them. I am responsible before God to teach them God's Word because they are to be the next God-fearing generation!

CHAPTER 4

WORDS THAT KILL
WORDS THAT GIVE LIFE

Death and life are in the power of the tongue,
and those who love it will eat its fruit.

PROVERBS 18:21

A short, feisty, down-to-earth, straightforward-talking New Yorker—that was my mother. She was extremely hardworking and kept late hours at the Union Bank in Los Angeles. Now imagine her with my dad—a Mexican who constantly drank. As a result, between them there would be knock-down, drag-out fights. My mom suffered tremendously because of my dad's drinking. He abused her verbally, emotionally and physically. Neither of my parents knew Christ, and they eventually divorced. Years later, they remarried; both of them came to Christ, and they remained inseparable—until death parted them.

Looking back, growing up in an abusive home was very difficult. As a child, even though I hated all the drinking and abuse in my home—when I grew up and eventually married, I also became abusive toward my wife. This is why I find it so hard to understand how Christian marriages can become abusive. There are husbands and wives who know what the Scriptures say about marriage, yet they refuse to obey God's Word. Instead, they make the choice to verbally, emotionally and physically abuse their spouses—sad.

A marriage relationship is severely damaged when a spouse uses abusive and deceptive language. Wives have said to me that unkind, hurtful words can be more damaging to them than any physical blow. Bruises fade, but the hurt feelings will remain in the heart. Words matter!

WORDS OF HYPOCRISY

Do you know that God hears every idle word we speak? We will give an account on Judgment Day for the words we have spoken to each other:

> *"But I say to you that for every idle word men may speak, they will give account of it in the day of judgment. For by your words you will be justified, and by your words you will be condemned."*
>
> MATTHEW 12:36–37

This is what Jesus said when He warned the Pharisees during His earthly ministry. As religious leaders of the day, they studied the Scriptures and seemed spiritual, but they were evil. Jesus told them they would be held accountable for their hypocritical and deceptive words unless they humbled themselves and repented.

When the sin of hypocrisy exists in a marriage relationship, it will create serious problems. At times, I have seen from my office window married couples arriving to church being rude to each other. Yet when they come through the front doors of the chapel, they are all smiles. In reality, they are being deceptive. A husband or wife can act spiritual at church, but be a completely different person at home.

It is important to realize that your family can see how you treat each other in private—at home. There are husbands and even wives who are disrespecting each other in front of their innocent children. A spouse can be argumentative, proud and unforgiving.

Today, marriage vows are not being honored. Quite the opposite, they are being dishonored, especially in the way married couples treat each other. Husbands and wives begin their married life making a promise to love, honor and cherish their spouses for as long as they live. Are those vows being kept in the words they now use?

When a spouse begins to use words that are disrespectful, the other spouse will feel unloved. The obvious danger is the temptation for a husband or wife to look in other places for comfort and affection—tearing the marriage apart. It is good to examine your marriage. What are you saying to each other? Seriously, there needs to be a mutual respect for one another—in doing so, choose your words wisely.

Go back to the first time you met your wife, when you were single, and you were both attracted to each other. Do you remember meeting her parents and humbly asking her father for permission to take her out on a date? As a gentleman, before you sat down in your car, you opened the door for her first. Whenever you entered a place, it was always ladies first. All these actions were done to show her respect and to win her heart. In your mind you were thinking, *This is the one I am going to marry; this woman is the one for me. I will love her, and she will love me.*

When you marry and vow to love one another, your actions should continue to show love and respect for one another throughout your marriage and not slip into a hypocritical relationship.

A SPIRIT-FILLED MARRIAGE

Marriage is not only a physical relationship; it is a spiritual relationship. Each spouse must be obedient to God's Word and live in the power of the Holy Spirit for their marriage to work.

When a couple first unites in marriage, they experience a time of happiness as newlyweds. They soon realize that marriage is not always smiling and saying, "I love you." The honeymoon stage comes to an end, and the couple will have to build their relationship on the Word of God.

In fact, it does not matter how long a couple has been together or whatever stage of life they find themselves in, all married couples have to work daily on their marriages. Fulfilled marriages are not automatic because we can be imperfect, selfish, and harsh. If a husband's or wife's relationship with God is not right, then their relationship with each other will not be, either. Think about that. When you are having disunity and stress as a couple, there will be no peace—both of you will constantly be at war. A married couple cannot function when there is no unity in the marriage; there will always be problems. How can each of them make sure their relationship with God is in right standing?

The Apostle Paul gave Christians important instructions on how they can work on their individual lives:

> . . . *walk in the Spirit, and you shall not fulfill the lust of the flesh. For the flesh lusts against the Spirit, and the Spirit against the flesh; and these are contrary to one another, so that you do not do the things that you wish.*
>
> GALATIANS 5:16–17

Paul taught in Ephesians 5:18, *be filled with the Spirit.* Having a Spirit-filled marriage does not mean you are not going to have problems. Men and women are still carrying around the *old man*—the flesh—having carnal desires. The reality is every marriage has problems, but when two people are walking in the Spirit, they can settle their problems spiritually and peacefully by using biblical principles.

Those who are having major problems in their marriage often seek marriage counseling. Some husbands and wives choose to pay for expensive marriage counseling, when it has been freely given to us in the Word of God. Often, married couples come into the chapel for counseling, pointing fingers at each other, instead of seeking to resolve their issues biblically.

In a marriage relationship, there must be humility, brokenness and true repentance. If a spouse is at fault, they should lay aside their pride and humbly take the blame. They should honestly admit, "I am the problem." Yet it seems so hard for husbands and wives to confess their faults to each other. If a married couple is truly Spirit-filled, then they will be able to correct the problem by obeying the Word of God. It is as simple as that!

As Christians—children of the Light—we are not like the people in the world. The Holy Spirit dwells in us. He will convict us of sin and enable us to have a Spirit-filled marriage.

THE ART OF COMMUNICATION

Good communication in a marriage relationship is crucial. Marriage is all about communication. As a couple, do you take time to sit and talk with each other? Marriage is hard work. A couple needs to make the effort to spend quality time together to express their thoughts and ideas. Marriages break apart because the husband and wife fail to communicate with each other.

TAKE CARE OF SMALL ISSUES

There will be issues that arise in your marriage that seem relatively small, but you still need to talk over these matters together. If a married couple ignores small, annoying problems, they will unfortunately end up being bigger issues, especially when no one is willing to work things out. That is why they must be taken care of right from the beginning. Each person needs to resolve issues till both partners are satisfied.

When two people are becoming acquainted with each other, they talk about big issues: how many children they want to have, where they desire to live, their personal goals in their careers, and their finances. All these subjects are addressed together to be sure they are on the same page. These are important discussions to have, but other, smaller topics also need to be discussed.

If you are already married, you may remember talking about where you wanted to live, but not where you wanted to be living after five or ten years. You may have discussed finances and who would handle the money, but never talked about how much money you would spend on gifts for family and friends or how much you would give in tithing or to charity. You may have decided on having three children, but not what you would do if you were not able to have children.

Arguments are often the result of allowing the small issues in your marriage to become mountains that you find difficult to overcome. I encourage you as a married couple to spend time in God's Word and in prayer. It is important to spend personal time alone with God, but it is equally important to spend time with Him together. When you take time together with the Lord, you will grow closer to Him and closer to each other, and you will be in one mind spiritually.

A Christian couple should be spiritually united in order to handle the things that come up in a marriage. When two people are walking together as one in the Lord, it is easier to work through both small problems and big problems.

Difficult situations can arise because of a couple's lack of communication. Husbands and wives are so busy that they no longer take time to communicate with each other. One thing is for sure—men and women communicate differently. Problems can be created when something said between a husband and wife is not clarified and talked over.

At times, when an innocent comment is made, a spouse may respond, "What did you mean by that?" There may be no hidden meaning. The spouse should not read more into a statement than what is actually being said. Husbands and wives need to avoid jumping to conclusions. It is so easy to make false assumptions—they must take words at face value and not look for hidden messages. If two people love and trust one another, they should give their spouse the benefit of the doubt. Healthy communication is vital for a good marriage.

THE SILENT TREATMENT

When a marriage partner has been offended by their spouse's words, they may respond with what is commonly known as *the silent treatment*. A wife or husband may decide not to speak to their spouse for days, weeks or even months. The Word of God tells us: *Be angry, and do not sin: do not let the sun go down on your wrath, nor give place to the devil* (Ephesians 4:26–27).

The most important thing to remember when arguing is when to end it. Do not hold a grudge or prolong the silent treatment. Speak your opinion and respect your spouse's opinion. Sometimes, you may have to agree to disagree to have peace in your home.

What happens when the communication is cut? Seriously, if a husband and wife fail to communicate, Satan will attempt to bring a wedge between them to separate them. It is best to resolve marital issues quickly. A couple should seek to restore communication and unity in their marriage so as not to give Satan a foothold in their relationship.

There are Christians whose marriages are thrashed because of the lack of communication—they each go their own separate ways, and neither is doing anything about it.

Clearly couples need to communicate. They must avoid hurting each other by ignoring a conflict and not speaking to each other about it. Unresolved situations will fester, and if left unsettled, the relationship will be broken—ending in divorce. Break the silence and talk it through.

WORDS OF TRANSFORMATION

The Apostle Paul, named Saul before his conversion, persecuted the Church. His words were filled with malice against Christians:

> . . . *Saul, still breathing threats and murder against the disciples of the Lord, went to the high priest and asked letters from him to the synagogues of Damascus, so that if he found any who were of the Way* [Believers in Christ], *whether men or women, he might bring them bound to Jerusalem.*
>
> ACTS 9:1–2

Paul's life was transformed when he came to Christ. Instead of persecuting and tearing down the Church with his words, Paul was used by God for the rest of his life to build up believers, by writing many important letters to the Church.

Paul instructed Christians in Colossians 3:8 on how their behavior needed to change. He told them, *put off all these: anger, wrath, malice, blasphemy, filthy language out of your mouth.* As our lives are transformed by Christ, so must our words change. Words spoken out of anger and filthy words can only cause hurt feelings and division between married couples. Common sense tells us those things are not edifying.

The words we speak and the actions we take are very significant. As a husband, if you speak to your wife using filthy language, angry, abusive words, or discouraging words to put her down, you are showing her that you do not love her. Likewise, if a wife speaks disrespectfully to her husband, she is not honoring him. What a man or woman says to each other has great consequence. I believe this with all my heart.

I have heard from couples who have had similar difficulties that my wife and I have experienced. As a man, I know I am not always sensitive to my wife's feelings. There are times when she gets upset with me, and I do not realize that something I said or did was hurtful to her. It could be because I spoke in a certain tone or I had a bad attitude. It may not have been anything to do with my words, but only the way I said them.

I honestly think there are times when men, including myself, are at a loss as to how we have offended our wives. There are other times when we do know, and we are guilty of purposely saying hurtful words.

Spouses should not bring up past hurts if they have already been resolved. This also ruins the marriage—it is like poison—you cannot do that. Does Christ do that to you? No! Once you repent and ask for forgiveness, Christ cleanses and washes you, and then you can go forward. It is the same with your marriage. When there is repentance and things in the past are settled, then there can be forgiveness, and your marriage can move forward. Ruth Bell Graham, wife of evangelist Billy Graham, said, "A good marriage is the union of two good forgivers." Right words can transform your marriage.

WORDS OF UNDERSTANDING

The Apostle Peter, in 1 Peter 3:1–7, instructed wives and husbands about their roles in their marriages. He wrote the first six verses to women, and only this one incredible verse to the men:

> *Husbands, likewise, dwell with them with understanding, giving honor to the wife, as to the weaker vessel, and as being heirs together of the grace of life, that your prayers may not be hindered.*

1 PETER 3:7

Notice, Peter gave important admonitions to Christian husbands. He exhorted them to treat their wives with understanding and honor, acknowledging the wife is the *weaker vessel*. It is not that the woman is weak, but she is weaker than the man. This could be because women are more emotional and sensitive than men, so their feelings are hurt more easily. So husbands are to love their wives and protect them.

If a husband does not treat his wife with understanding and honor, his prayers will be hindered. It could be very possible that some husbands are not having any results in their prayer life. Their prayers have been literally cut off from the Lord because they are treating their wives unkindly.

TENDERNESS, LOVE AND AFFECTION

As a Christian husband, you have to care about your relationship with your wife. Women like to be told they are loved; they like tenderness—affection.

In our marriages, we have to accept how God created men and women differently. In His Word, God gave them each different responsibilities. God has instructed husbands that they need to be understanding with their wives and be sensitive to their emotional needs. Seriously, at times I find it hard to deal with my wife's needs—we are so different. I can get into a car and say, "Man, it is hot in here." Then she will say, "It is freezing cold." Different!

I am a very hard-core and difficult person to live with. I am still learning to be a husband—I am not a perfect husband but I do know what the Scriptures teach, and I am seeking to obey them. It is by the grace of God that I am the person that I am today.

One thing I want to confess to you—straight out. I do not like holding my wife's hand in public or any type of public affection. I guess that is something I grew up with. I show my wife affection privately. I see men wrapped around their wives—and their wives love that. Yet I would feel embarrassed. Some people are naturally affectionate, and God honors those actions of love towards their wives.

It is important for husbands to understand that God has given them a gift from heaven—a wife—and she needs to be treated and handled with care:

> *Every good gift and every perfect gift is from above, and comes down from the Father of lights, with whom there is no variation or shadow of turning.*
>
> JAMES 1:17

COMPANIONSHIP

The Scriptures teach us to enjoy each other's companionship. It can be a difficult thing to do; the men go to work, and young wives are at home with their children all day long. As a mother, she has been busy taking the older kids to school, while talking baby talk to her younger children, clothing and feeding them, changing diapers, and cleaning the house.

A wife sees her husband coming home from work and gets excited. In her mind, she is thinking, *I am going to get to talk to him, be with him, and share what has gone on in the day.* She anticipates adult conversation with her husband—someone to speak to on her own level. The wife desires intelligent conversation with her husband—his companionship.

Now imagine, a husband walks through the door tired. He tells her, "Do not talk to me right now; leave me alone. I was on the freeway for one hour, and I had a bad day at the office." The husband plants himself on the couch, turns on the television, and listens to sports.

He never talks to his wife. Men have the tendency to be rough, cold and distracted by sports, fishing and other hobbies—they can become very neglectful. This is why it is important to both discuss and agree when the best time is to communicate. A wife needs to use wisdom as to the right time to enjoy companionship with her husband, and not to expect his immediate attention when he walks through the door, worn out.

On the other hand, husbands also need to be sensitive and make time to speak to their wives; otherwise, someone else will talk to her! When that happens, do not be surprised if she gets a boyfriend and leaves you. That is just the truth—that is what happens in marriages—so sad.

Many older men can come to a place where they stop caring and talking to their wives. They get a real bad attitude towards them, they shut down, and they tune out their wives—just ignore them. Both husband and wife must seek each other's companionship to have an inseparable union.

THE POWER OF WORDS

King Solomon understood the power of words. He proclaimed: *Death and life are in the power of the tongue, and those who love it will eat its fruit* (Proverbs 18:21). The words we say to one another have great power. Words can either build up or tear down. They can encourage and bring peace, or bring discouragement and depression. Seriously, what comes out of our mouths can inflict wounds or bring healing: *The words of a man's mouth are deep waters; the wellspring of wisdom is a flowing brook* (Proverbs 18:4).

Throughout the book of Proverbs, Solomon penned much wisdom and knowledge. If only a husband and wife will choose to apply the wisdom of Solomon's words to their relationship, they will greatly benefit from the fruit of it.

Solomon had great insight into what happens in a marriage relationship. As kings did in those days, and contrary to God's Word, he accumulated 700 wives and 300 concubines. It seemed as if he lived with many contentious women who caused strife:

> *. . . the contentions of a wife are a continual dripping* (Proverbs 19:13).

> *Better to dwell in a corner of a housetop, than in a house shared with a contentious woman* (Proverbs 21:9).

> *Better to dwell in the wilderness, than with a contentious and angry woman* (Proverbs 21:19).

The virtuous woman—a woman of valor—is completely opposite to the contentious woman. It is believed by theologians that Bathsheba, wife of King David, was the one who wrote of the wisdom of finding a virtuous wife to her son King Solomon. She began her instruction first with a good question and spoke of her worth, describing her fruitful virtues. She knew a virtuous woman would benefit her son and many others in her sphere of influence:

> *Who can find a virtuous wife? For her worth is far above rubies. The heart of her husband safely trusts her; so he will have no lack of gain. She does him good and not evil all the days of her life.*
>
> PROVERBS 31:10–12

A husband's heart is safe with a virtuous woman because she does him good and not evil. This woman also understands the power of words: *She opens her mouth with wisdom, and on her tongue is the law of kindness* (Proverbs 31:26). She guards her words against saying anything to purposely bring pain and hurt to her husband or her children, but seeks to speak God's wisdom to them.

A virtuous woman is a crown to her husband: *An excellent wife is* the crown of her hu*sband*... (Proverbs 12:4). The crown is a symbol of honor and nobility: *Her husband is known in the gates, when he sits among the elders of the land* (Proverbs 31:23). Her wisdom and influence causes her husband to become respected in society—a place of prominence.

James, the brother of Jesus, warned about the negative effects of the power of the tongue:

> *Even so the tongue is a little member and boasts great things. See how great a forest a little fire kindles! And the tongue is a fire, a world of iniquity. The tongue is so set among our members that it defiles the whole body, and sets on fire the course of nature; and it is set on fire by hell.*
>
> JAMES 3:5–6

The tongue is a very small part of our bodies, and yet it can do great damage. It can defile the entire body if we use it with evil intent. James went on to explain how the tongue can be used for good or for evil; we make the choice:

> *With it we bless our God and Father, and with it we curse men, who have been made in the similitude of God. Out of the same mouth proceed blessing and cursing. My brethren, these things ought not to be so.*
>
> JAMES 3:9–10

REFRAIN YOUR TONGUE FROM EVIL

Christian couples have a responsibility to follow after Christ. He is the standard. As we imitate Christ, our lives will become transformed. As followers of Christ, we have our Lord as an example of how we are to treat one another. It is not a suggestion; it is a command. Jesus said: *A new commandment I give to you, that you love one another; as I have loved you, that you also love one another* (John 13:34).

If we want to obey God's command to love one another, we will speak words of love to build each other up and not tear each other down. In our tongues, we have the power of good and the power of evil. We have to choose how we want to use this tiny member of the body. God's love will be evident in our lives by the way we speak to each other. If we choose to bless with the words we speak, God will bless us, and He will hear our prayers:

> For "He who would love life and see good days, let him refrain his tongue from evil, and his lips from speaking deceit. Let him turn away from evil and do good; let him seek peace and pursue it. For the eyes of the Lord are on the righteous, and His ears are open to their prayers; but the face of the Lord is against those who do evil."
>
> 1 PETER 3:10–12

As a pastor, I have to apply God's Word to my own marriage. When Sharon and I have had disagreements, we had to work through them through the Scriptures. When my wife and I are not in agreement, I must turn to them for wisdom, and I have been encouraged and exhorted through it.

In 1 Corinthians 13, Paul described the love God desires that we have for one another. Loving my wife as the Lord desires is very important because it is a reflection of my relationship with Him. When seeking the Lord for my marriage, I am reminded to put my name in place of the word *love* in 1 Corinthians 13:4–8, to see if I am living up to the standard that God wants from me:

> *Love* [Raul] *suffers long and is kind; love* [Raul] *does not envy; love* [Raul] *does not parade itself, is not puffed up; does not behave rudely, does not seek its own, is not provoked, thinks no evil; does not rejoice in iniquity, but rejoices in the truth; bears all things, believes all things, hopes all things, endures all things. Love* [Raul] *never fails.*

If I cannot put my name in any part of these verses, I know I have to humble myself before God. I certainly do not want my prayers to be hindered, and I want to always have free access to the Lord, without any barriers. As we surrender to God, He will help us to bring life into our marriages by using our tongues in a way that is pleasing to Him.

CHAPTER 5

TRUSTING GOD AS YOU WAIT

So Abraham said to the oldest servant of his house, who ruled over all that he had, "Please, put your hand under my thigh, and I will make you swear by the LORD, the God of heaven and the God of the earth, that you will not take a wife for my son from the daughters of the Canaanites, among whom I dwell . . .

GENESIS 24:2–3

God ordained marriage. The LORD had a plan for Adam before Eve was even created. Man was alone, so God, knowing exactly what he needed, created a woman and brought her to the man to be his wife (Genesis 2:22). It is important to point out, Adam did not go looking for a wife; God brought her to him.

God saw the loneliness of Adam and made Eve specifically for him. If God has plans for you to marry, He will bring into your life the exact person He has chosen for you. This is the biblical way.

Just as Eve was made a helpmate for Adam and his companion for life, God wants to bring to you your spouse, someone to be your companion—a best friend to remain united—inseparable for the rest of your life.

Do you remember Adam's response when God brought Eve to him? Adam said: *"This is now bone of my bones and flesh of my flesh; she shall be called Woman, because she was taken out of Man"* (Genesis 2:23). He was incredibly happy with God's amazing gift to him. If you wait on the Lord, you will be also. So let God choose your spouse!

PRAYING FOR A SPOUSE

God desires to bless single Christians who are longing to marry with the person He has chosen. You do not need to go looking for a husband or a wife. If you want to have a lasting marriage, begin by laying a spiritual foundation, seeking God's will for your future spouse in prayer.

Why is it important to seek the Lord for your future spouse through prayer? God is omniscient—all-knowing—which means He knows each person's heart and soul. God alone knows who will be the perfect match for you. He will be faithful to direct your life as you pray.

Only the Lord can give you the desire of your heart. As you pray, He prepares your heart to be aligned with His perfect will. Your desire will become His plan for your life.

This truth is reflected in Psalm 37:4–5: *Delight yourself also in the Lord, and He shall give you the desires of your heart. Commit your way to the Lord, trust also in Him, and He shall bring it to pass.*

I believe with all my heart that as you wait on God's timing to bring you a spouse, you need to spend your time wisely—praying, studying God's Word, and serving Him. Jesus taught believers their first priority: *"But seek first the kingdom of God and His righteousness, and all these things shall be added to you"* (Matthew 6:33). Keep yourself busy serving the Lord.

LONELINESS

When a single person becomes lonely, God sees and understands. He wants to first fill their loneliness with Himself—His companionship. God does not want them to suddenly rush out and marry just anybody.

When that happens, they can make a serious mistake, resulting in tragic consequences.

There are many lonely single Christians who have become impatient. Instead of praying and waiting on God for a spouse, they willfully make their own choice without asking God for His wisdom. They take the matter into their own hands. Christians must avoid making this mistake; make sure you are obeying God's Word.

During your season of singleness, allow God to prepare your heart, so when the time comes, you are ready to be married. In His perfect way, and in His perfect timing, God will unite a man and a woman together.

SINGLENESS AND DATING

Christians should not be dating for fun or out of loneliness—that can be unfulfilling and dangerous. Many single people who habitually date get themselves into trouble. They suffer temptation and, as a result, fall into sexual sin. Self-control is very hard; it can only be accomplished through the power of the Holy Spirit: *Walk in the Spirit, and you shall not fulfill the lust of the flesh. But the fruit of the Spirit is . . . self-control* (Galatians 5:16, 22, 23).

We live in a different era. In hopes of finding marital bliss, single Christians seek companionship via social media. It has become another area of temptation for single people. How many Christians today visit dating websites? They search for their "perfect match." The chances are very slim. Can a single person really find God's perfect will by looking for a spouse online? They hope to find a fulfilling relationship. No possible way! Relationships such as these are usually short-lived. However, if a commitment is made and they do marry, will they keep their marital vows made before God? Single people, you cannot help God out! Let Him do the finding.

Sadly, there are accounts of people who have experienced disappointment after seeking companionship online. They have suffered because of a failed promise and no commitment. Scary stories have been told about people who met predators online. Strangers with ulterior motives have robbed them, demanded sex, or even worse. It could be they thought they were going to meet the person of their dreams, but they ended up brutally murdered.

Online dating is a multibillion dollar industry in the US. How would you know if the person you are engaging in conversation with is not lying about who they really are? Are they married? A sex offender? Underage? Each year there are thousands of abductions, rapes and hundreds of murders due to online dating.

Be careful! You are taking a risk. It is crucial to your emotional and spiritual life to surrender to God and trust Him to fulfill His purposes in your life. God can direct you to meet the one who fits His plan for you. Believe the promise of Jeremiah 29:11: *For I know the thoughts that I think toward you* [intricate plans], *says the* Lord, *thoughts of peace and not of evil, to give you a future and a hope.*

Consider that the person *you* desire to spend your life with may not be God's choice. The Lord knows your life from the very beginning to the very end. Trust Him—wait on Him to bring His plans to pass.

OUTWARD APPEARANCES

Single Christians might be tempted to look at the outward appearance of a person. They desire someone who is sexually attractive to them as the perfect choice for a spouse. Never be moved by the desire to please your flesh—carnal desires.

I have heard men say, "I am praying God brings me a woman like a fashion model. She has to look good in a bikini." It is not only men who do this. Women can pray the same way, "Lord, please bring me a tall, dark and handsome man." Both men and women try to tell God exactly what they would like in a spouse physically. It is a big mistake to focus only on a person's physical appearance. A single Christian should be more concerned with the spiritual condition of a potential spouse. It is more important to seek God's will and not your own. Consider this: God is more concerned with the heart—the inner person.

However, I believe Christian men and women alike should take care of their physical bodies. They must outshine the people in the world—in appearance, behavior and wisdom. They are to be the most beautiful people on earth.

When God wanted to choose a new king for Israel, the qualifying factor was found in his heart, not his outward appearance. When the prophet Samuel was sent by the LORD to anoint one of Jesse's sons to be the next king, he made the mistake of looking at the eldest son's outward appearance. He saw Eliab's impressive stature—tall and handsome—and said: *"Surely the LORD's anointed is before Him."* The LORD corrected Samuel's thinking:

> *"Do not look at his appearance or at his physical stature, because I have refused him. For the LORD does not see as man sees; for man looks at the outward appearance, but the LORD looks at the heart."*
>
> 1 SAMUEL 16:7

Only God can truly know the heart of a person. Single people have a tendency to look at the physical appearance of a potential spouse; they overlook the heart and spiritual condition of a person. This is the reason single Christians need to hear from God and know His will before they get married. They need to make sure to marry the right person. It is very serious when you make a vow for marriage before God. It is a lifetime commitment.

Everyone has been created by God with a free will. We are not robots. Single people are never forced to accept God's will for their lives, and they have the freedom to seek their own desires. However, if they marry out of God's will, God, in His mercy and grace, can restore a failing marriage relationship as they each seek the Lord.

CONTENTMENT IN SINGLENESS

There are those who have been single for a long time who are absolutely miserable. It could be they feel the stigma of not being married. Or they are wondering, *What is wrong with me? Why has God not brought someone into my life?* Seek the Lord earnestly, truthfully, with all your heart. It could be God wants you to continue to wait, or He may have chosen for you to remain single, at which time, He would give you contentment, He would take away your desire to be married, and you would be fulfilled in your single life.

In fact, Christ would become your *All in All,* your Partner for life. I know, and have worked with, those who fully love and serve the Lord without the desire to get married; they are completely satisfied with what God has determined for them. For those longing to share their lives with another person in marriage, God's Word has principles to follow to keep you in His perfect will while you wait.

The Apostle Paul, as a Pharisee, would likely have been married. In ministry, as a believer in Christ, he somehow became single. Either His wife died, or his wife left him; we do not really know, but he stayed single all of his life. Paul gave believers godly advice concerning singleness:

> *But I say this as a concession, not as a commandment. For I wish that all men were even as I myself. But each one has his own gift from God, one in this manner and another in that. But I say to the unmarried and to the widows: It is good for them if they remain even as I am; but if they cannot exercise self-control, let them marry. For it is better to marry than to burn with passion.*
>
> 1 CORINTHIANS 7:6–9

Paul spoke from personal experience about the obvious cares of marriage that can make serving the Lord, at times, more difficult:

> *But I want you to be without care. He who is unmarried cares for the things of the Lord—how he may please the Lord. But he who is married cares about the things of the world—how he may please his wife. There is a difference between a wife and a virgin. The unmarried woman cares about the things of the Lord, that she may be holy both in body and in spirit. But she who is married cares about the things of the world—how she may please her husband. And this I say for your own profit, not that I may put a leash on you, but for what is proper, and that you may serve the Lord without distraction.*
>
> 1 CORINTHIANS 7:32–35

John Wesley taught: "The single life is about undistracted holiness." There are many people who live contented lives for God in undistracted holiness. Autobiographies have been written of missionaries who lived fulfilled lives serving the Lord on the mission field, like Amy Carmichael, who never married; she served the Lord in India for 55 years. Gladys Aylward willfully and sacrificially spent her lifetime in China, while David Brainerd, in his service to the Lord, preached to the native Indians and, joyfully and literally, exhausted himself to death as a missionary.

Paul also gave practical life principles to Timothy, a young minister, who he considered a son in the faith: *Now godliness with contentment is great gain* (1 Timothy 6:6). Paul also shared with him, *I have learned in whatever state I am, to be content* (Philippians 4:11).

Although these passages are not in regard to singleness, these principles are helpful to someone struggling with not being married. If they serve the Lord with all their hearts, they will find contentment as they wait patiently for Him to bring them a spouse.

KEEP BIBLICAL BOUNDARIES

God's Word, when obeyed, will guide a single person. When God brings two people together, their relationship needs to be kept pure before the marriage takes place. It needs to be based on the foundation of Christ—holy.

It is important to keep biblical boundaries to ensure a couple remains pure before the Lord. I believe with all my heart it is best not to be together alone. Never place yourselves in a situation of temptation, where you both could fall into sexual sin—fornication. In avoiding temptation, the man needs to take the leadership in the relationship by praying with the woman he is dating. They should read the Scriptures together, which many times is lacking in relationships. Purity in a relationship stems from a couple's spirituality. A couple must examine their commitment to Jesus Christ. If they really want holiness, they need to obey God's Word. Then He will bless their relationship.

God will not bless a couple's relationship if they are breaking His Word by having sex before marriage. Paul warned believers of the serious consequences of engaging in premarital sex: *Flee sexual immorality. Every sin that a man does is outside the body, but he who commits sexual immorality sins against his own body* (1 Corinthians 6:18).

God never intended for men and women to have sex before marriage. If you find yourself being pressured into having sex, break the relationship, because it is not based on love, but on lust. If a single couple is continuously having sexual intercourse, there is a real risk of not having a good marriage in the future. You must build your relationship on a spiritual foundation—on the Rock—Jesus Christ.

When an unmarried couple comes to me for advice with the desire to get married, and they are in sexual sin or living together in sin, I will not marry them. I strongly advise them to separate for a time, so they can get their individual lives right before the Lord. They need to deny their flesh and lustful passion.

A couple should wait to see if they are truly in love with each other and whether their relationship is really from the Lord. As they go to church, read the Bible, and pray separately for a time, the Lord will speak to their hearts, individually. They must allow the Lord to do a work in each of their lives. Then if the Lord confirms they are to be together, they can continue to build a new foundation led by the Spirit of God.

Timothy was a young pastor, and Paul, as a father, took him under his wing. He encouraged Timothy, giving him valuable, spiritual advice: *Let no one despise your youth, but be an example to the believers in word, in conduct, in love, in spirit, in faith, in purity* (1 Timothy 4:12). As a youth, he was to be morally pure and a good example to others.

Knowing God desires purity, if you cannot control your passions, and you are tempted to sin, remember, God designed for a man and woman to be married, to avoid fornication. When you are tempted sexually, come to the Cross of Jesus Christ and be obedient to the Word of God. Pray for a wife or husband so you can be married. Paul explains:

> *Now concerning the things of which you wrote to me: It is good for a man not to touch a woman. Nevertheless, because*

of sexual immorality, let each man have his own wife, and let each woman have her own husband.

1 CORINTHIANS 7:1–2

Many young people have embraced the worldly philosophy of sexual freedom and have abandoned morality. They live very loose lives. It is hard to find anyone who has not had sex before marriage. Consequently, people have become very disappointed. Those who have saved themselves for marriage will find a greater sexual fulfillment for waiting. As a pastor, I challenge young adults not to have a serious relationship until they are ready to be married.

Those who date casually are placing themselves in a dangerous position to fall into sexual sin. It is not of the Lord to *play the field*— dating for fun. Many single people have messed around sexually and lost their virginity and innocent purity. Do not play with sex; you will get burned—big time. Not only that, you will hurt others. Women are often left by their boyfriends to become single mothers. Some women are afraid and choose to end the life of their child. Children are gifts from God. In sincere repentance, a woman can be forgiven, but she cannot continue to willfully sin sexually.

It is good to see people take godly advice, keep themselves pure, dedicate their lives to the Lord, and wait on Him. Then, at the right time, He will bring the person He has prepared for them from before all eternity. When this happens, the relationship is to be kept pure. They should avoid kissing. A couple will become involved on a deeper, emotional level; their hormones will be out of control. Kissing will most likely lead to sex!

I respect my son Ryan's decision, once he came back to the Lord; he made a stand, vowing he would abstain from sex until God brought him his wife. He kept to the biblical way—purity. As he waited, the Lord greatly blessed him.

Humorously, as my granddaughters reach the age when they have boyfriends, believe me, I will be sharpening my Samurai sword! Seriously, I will be sharing with all six of them the importance of waiting on the Lord—I want them to be blessed with God's best.

A WIFE FOR ISAAC

We have an incredible story in Genesis 24 of Abraham who was one of the most blessed men living in the world. The LORD gave him a son in his old age, and when Abraham was older, and Sarah his wife had passed away, he saw Isaac's need for a wife. Since they lived among idolatrous foreigners, Abraham wanted to be sure his son married from among his family—in the will of God. Abraham gave the task of finding Isaac a wife to his oldest servant:

> *Now Abraham was old, well advanced in age; and the LORD had blessed Abraham in all things. So Abraham said to the oldest servant of his house, who ruled over all that he had, "Please, put your hand under my thigh, and I will make you swear by the LORD, the God of heaven and the God of the earth, that you will not take a wife for my son from the daughters of the Canaanites, among whom I dwell; but you shall go to my country and to my family, and take a wife for my son Isaac."*
> GENESIS 24:1–4

According to the Jewish customs of that time, this was how promises were made—vows. It is also important to understand the typology seen in Abraham's search for a wife for his son, Isaac. Abraham is a type of God the Father who longs for His Son to be united to the Church—the Bride of Christ. Isaac is a type of God's Son waiting for His Bride—the Church. Abraham's servant is a type of the Holy Spirit who seeks out those who will be joined to God's Son, who make up the Church. Believers are a type of the Bride of Christ.

Abraham was trusting in the LORD as he sent his servant to find a bride for Isaac. He had faith that God would guide his servant. Yet the servant became anxious about failing his master, so he asked Abraham: *"Perhaps the woman will not be willing to follow me to this land. Must I take your son back to the land from which you came?"* (Genesis 24:5). Abraham was not worried about the woman not following his servant. God was in control of the situation. He encouraged his servant with the promise God had given him:

> *But Abraham said to him, "Beware that you do not take my son back there. The LORD God of heaven, who took me from my father's house and from the land of my family, and who spoke to me and swore to me, saying, 'To your descendants I give this land,' He will send His angel before you, and you shall take a wife for my son from there. And if the woman is not willing to follow you, then you will be released from this oath; only do not take my son back there."*
>
> GENESIS 24:6–8

The servant trusted his master, agreed to do what was asked of him, and departed for Mesopotamia. As the servant came near to the city, he prayed to the LORD. He knew the only way he could succeed was through God's divine intervention. He wanted God to give him a sign, so he would know God's will:

> *So the servant put his hand under the thigh of Abraham his master, and swore to him concerning this matter. Then the servant took ten of his master's camels and departed, for all his master's goods were in his hand. And he arose and went to Mesopotamia, to the city of Nahor. And he made his camels kneel down outside the city by a well of water at evening time, the time when women go out to draw water. Then he said, "O LORD God of my master Abraham, please give me success this day, and show kindness to my master Abraham. Behold, here I stand by the well of water, and the daughters of the men of the*

city are coming out to draw water. Now let it be that the young woman to whom I say, 'Please let down your pitcher that I may drink,' and she says, 'Drink, and I will also give your camels a drink'—let her be the one You have appointed for Your servant Isaac. And by this I will know that You have shown kindness to my master."

GENESIS 24:9–14

If all these things took place, Abraham's servant would know without a doubt that the woman was sent to him by the LORD. Before the servant finished praying, the LORD sent Rebekah out to the well; she was the first to come:

And it happened, before he had finished speaking, that behold, Rebekah, who was born to Bethuel, son of Milcah, the wife of Nahor, Abraham's brother, came out with her pitcher on her shoulder. Now the young woman was very beautiful to behold, a virgin; no man had known her. And she went down to the well, filled her pitcher, and came up.

GENESIS 24:15–16

Everything happened in answer to the servant's prayer. He did not have to search and search for a bride for Isaac; God brought her to the servant, so he would have no doubt. The servant knew these circumstances were not a coincidence. With all the confirmation God provided for him, the servant boldly approached Rebekah and said:

"Please let me drink a little water from your pitcher." So she said, "Drink, my lord." Then she quickly let her pitcher down to her hand, and gave him a drink. And when she had finished giving him a drink, she said, "I will draw water for your camels also, until they have finished drinking." Then she quickly emptied her pitcher into the trough, ran back to the well to draw water, and drew for all his camels. And the man, wondering at her, remained silent so as to know whether the

Lord had made his journey prosperous or not. So it was, when the camels had finished drinking, that the man took a golden nose ring weighing half a shekel, and two bracelets for her wrists weighing ten shekels of gold, and said, "Whose daughter are you? Tell me, please, is there room in your father's house for us to lodge?" So she said to him, "I am the daughter of Bethuel, Milcah's son, whom she bore to Nahor." Moreover she said to him, "We have both straw and feed enough, and room to lodge." Then the man bowed down his head and worshiped the Lord.

GENESIS 24:17–26

The servant recognized the work of the Lord, and he gave Him all honor and glory. The woman God brought to him was a relative of Abraham. It was clear—God had provided a wife for Isaac.

And he said, "Blessed be the Lord God of my master Abraham, who has not forsaken His mercy and His truth toward my master. As for me, being on the way, the Lord led me to the house of my master's brethren." So the young woman ran and told her mother's household these things.

GENESIS 24:27–28

In verses 29–48, God brought the woman to Abraham's servant, and he put the nose ring on her nose and the two bracelets on her wrist. He bowed his head and worshiped the Lord. God prepared Rebekah's heart to receive his servant into her father's home. God honored his journey of faith. Rebekah introduced Abraham's servant to her family and explained what he had said to her. The servant related how Abraham his master had sent him to their country to find a wife for his son Isaac from among his family. He continued to discuss how he had prayed to the Lord, asking Him to reveal who He had chosen to be Isaac's wife. When Rebekah came to the well, she did everything he had prayed to the Lord about, and it was a sure confirmation that the Lord had led him.

When Abraham's servant ended his story, he asked permission to take Rebekah back with him to be Isaac's wife: *"Now if you will deal kindly and truly with my master, tell me. And if not, tell me, that I may turn to the right hand or to the left."* (Genesis 24:49).

After hearing his tremendous story, Rebekah's father Bethuel and her brother Laban could not deny the LORD's will:

> *Then Laban and Bethuel answered and said, "The thing comes from the LORD; we cannot speak to you either bad or good. Here is Rebekah before you; take her and go, and let her be your master's son's wife, as the LORD has spoken."*
>
> GENESIS 24:50–51

Rebekah's family recognized the hand of the LORD upon the entire situation and gave Rebekah to Abraham's servant to take her to Isaac. God's will was undeniable.

When Abraham's servant heard their response, he worshipped the LORD: *And it came to pass, when Abraham's servant heard their words, that he worshiped the LORD, bowing himself to the earth* (Genesis 24:52).

Imagine how happy he was to know Rebekah had her family's blessing in departing with him. Everything was going so smoothly—all according to God's will. There was no striving. The choice was now left with Rebekah. She chose not to linger, but immediately packed her things and left with the servant, taking her nurse and maids with her. As they drew near, Isaac was out in the field and saw them coming, so he went to meet them.

Meanwhile, Rebekah questioned who this man was. Finding out that it was Isaac, she covered herself with a veil (Genesis 24:53–65). Abraham's servant must have been so excited to share how the LORD prospered his journey:

And the servant told Isaac all the things that he had done. Then Isaac brought her into his mother Sarah's tent; and he took Rebekah and she became his wife, and he loved her. So Isaac was comforted after his mother's death.

GENESIS 24:66–67

Notice, even though Isaac had never seen or spoken to Rebekah, he submitted to the will of the LORD, opened his heart, and loved Rebekah. She was God's choice for him. God knew exactly who was a perfect helpmate for Isaac, and He brought her to him. In providing a wife for Isaac, God also gave comfort to him, because he was still grieved over the death of his mother.

Through Isaac and Rebekah's story, we can learn how God draws two people together. We see His faithfulness in revealing His will and guiding people as they pray. The exciting part is to see how God moves in answer to people's prayers. In doing so, He eliminates all doubt and confirms to their hearts His perfect plan. Truthfully, if single people trust God and obey His Word, He will divinely guide their steps and fulfill the desires of their hearts.

CHAPTER 6

UNEQUALLY YOKED

Do not be unequally yoked together with unbelievers. For what fellowship has righteousness with lawlessness? And what communion has light with darkness? And what accord has Christ with Belial? Or what part has a believer with an unbeliever?

2 CORINTHIANS 6:14–15

It is never God's will in any given situation to be unequally yoked—joined in a relationship or marriage with a nonbeliever. My wife can tell you from experience that when she became involved with me, a nonbeliever, then later united with me in marriage, she suffered tremendously for four-and-a-half years.

Though she was a Christian, she willingly chose to disobey what God had said in His Word, *Do not be unequally yoked together with unbelievers,* which caused Sharon to reap the consequences of her sin.

Even though I was raised in the Catholic church, I was a heathen, and my parents were nonbelievers. We had no relationship with the God of the Bible. However, Sharon's parents were godly people who had served God with all their hearts on the mission fields of Colombia and Chile.

Sharon had a unique life; she had been brought up on the mission field knowing God's Word, but in spite of this, she chose to have an intimate relationship with me. Sharon saw many people saved through her parents' ministry, so she believed firmly that one day I would get saved. As a couple, we were physically attracted to each other.

Forced apart, I was shipped to Vietnam to fight in the war. Once there, our relationship deepened as we communicated through letters. She would write me long letters, telling me about her God, and her desire to be a missionary. It did not bother me she was religious; I was a Catholic.

Absence made our feelings grow for each other until we fell in love. When I returned home, desperate to see each other, I sweet-talked her into having sex. Not waiting for marriage, we broke the law of God:

> *Do you not know that the unrighteous will not inherit the kingdom of God? Do not be deceived. Neither fornicators, nor idolaters, nor adulterers, nor homo- sexuals, nor sodomites, nor thieves, nor covetous, nor drunkards, nor revilers, nor extortioners will inherit the kingdom of God.*
>
> 1 CORINTHIANS 6:9–10

It is very clear; the Bible instructs that Christians should never date nonbelievers. If a believer chooses to ignore God's warnings, they will get hurt—they will get burned. In your heart, you may think you are going to "save" the nonbeliever, but you will be out of the will of God. Allow the Holy Spirit to work in their life. That is His work. You have been called to be obedient to the Word of God, which tells you not to be in an unequally yoked relationship—period.

Sharon, as a result of being intimate with me, became pregnant outside of marriage. She was strongly convicted because she knew she had sinned against God. She repented in humility and contrition:

> "I had broken my vow with God. All my life, I had made promises to the Lord, believing that in doing so, I would somehow prevent myself from disobeying Him. How could anyone break a promise to God? The fact was, I had managed to do it more often than I cared to recall. This time it was serious. I knew it was . . ."
>
> *My Husband My Maker*
> Sharon Faith Ries

After we married—unequally yoked and with our child—life was difficult. Sharon knew I was being unfaithful to her by committing adultery, and she suffered terrible verbal and physical abuse.

One day, God ministered to my wife as she stared at an old school picture of me as a little boy in a baseball outfit. Sharon heard the still, small voice of the Lord whisper to her broken heart, "Will you love him for me?" Sharon was committed to love me. In the end, God stepped into our situation, and four years later, by the grace of God I got saved.

LIGHT AND DARKNESS

The Apostle Paul, as a spiritual father, strongly exhorted the believers in Corinth. He wanted them to make sure they examined his Christian walk and his ministry so they could understand the grace of God in his life. Then they could comprehend through his exhortation how he wanted to extend to them the same grace—the unmerited favor of God—through the knowledge of the Gospel of Jesus Christ.

Like many Christians in our churches today, the Corinthians were spiritually immature and carnal. As believers, they were still ruled by their worldly desires, which caused them to have major problems in their lives. Paul knew the Corinthian believers lived among idolatrous people who worshiped idols. They defiled themselves with the worship of these sensual gods. Christians were in danger of being pulled away from their faith in Christ to worship false gods, when they intermarried or had close friendships with them. Paul firmly exhorted them *not to be unequally yoked together with unbelievers.*

Like the Corinthians, we also have to live in this idolatrous world among nonbelievers who do not know Christ. When I am around my nonbelieving friends it is for a good reason—to tell them about Jesus Christ. If you have friendships with nonbelievers, it is all right to spend time with them, but when they begin to do sinful things, make sure to remove yourself from them—separate. Seriously, cut them off, or they will cause you to stumble. You cannot party with them; otherwise, what kind of a witness would you be?

Christians are in the light; you cannot have close fellowship with those who are in the darkness. It is an impossibility. Understand, by having fellowship with them, you are actually having fellowship with Satan himself! Every person who does not have Christ is subject to Satan, and he is their father, whereas we have God as our Father. We are children of God, and we are to come out from among them:

> For what fellowship has righteousness with lawlessness? And what communion has light with darkness? And what accord has Christ with Belial? Or what part has a believer with an unbeliever? And what agreement has the temple of God with idols? For you are the temple of the living God. As God has said: "I will dwell in them and walk among them. I will be their God, and they shall be My people." Therefore "Come out from among them and be separate, says the Lord. Do not touch what is unclean, and I will receive you. I will be a Father to you, and you shall be My sons and daughters," says the Lord Almighty."
>
> 2 CORINTHIANS 6:14–18

Paul spoke to the Corinthians, and speaks to us, about close relationships: marriage, dating, friendships, and those in business. This applies to teenagers wanting a boyfriend or girlfriend, single adults who desire to be married, divorcees or widows wishing to remarry, friendships, and those seeking a partner in business. Paul urged believers to obey the Word of God and to stick to it without any compromise. It is all about submission to God—your will has to be in submission to God. If you do the will of God, then you will be blessed!

Christians should never choose to be in an unequally yoked relationship. We are the temple of the Living God! If God dwells in us, we cannot be in communion with nonbelievers. A believer in Christ should not marry someone who has a different doctrine or belief. A child of the Light should love all people and be the light in the darkness, but the Word of God forbids them to marry anyone who is in the darkness.

This is one area where young people, in particular, make great mistakes. Listen, if you are a teenager or young adult, and you are thinking about dating someone, it is important that you follow God's Word. Do not date a nonbeliever or be united with them. I think of all the young girls and men in the church who are out in the world attending colleges, high schools and junior high schools who are going against the Word of God by having a boyfriend or girlfriend who does not have a personal relationship with Jesus. It is only a matter of time before they bring you to a place of compromise. Instead of them becoming like Christ, you become like them—be careful. If you really want God's best for your life, read and obey the Bible.

If you are a single person dating a nonbeliever, then you are disobeying God and sinning against Him. How can you say you are *one* with them? You cannot! A Christian cannot be united together as *one* with a person who does not walk with God. They do not have Christ! Christians have nothing in common spiritually with nonbelievers. They have no true fellowship—absolutely nothing at all. A person without Christ will not have the same convictions, principles and morals that have been instilled in you as a child of God. The Word of God teaches Christians to *flee also youthful lusts; but pursue righteousness, faith, love, peace with those who call on the Lord out of a pure heart* (2 Timothy 2:22). A nonbeliever really has no interest in keeping God's Word.

PREGNANCY OUT OF MARRIAGE

When Sharon was pregnant before marriage her main preoccupation was to train up her child in the Lord, still having in mind ways to bring me to Christ. I was so excited about having a child; we soon married, and I took the responsibility for her and our son. We loved our first-born son, Raul Jr., and then we had two more sons, Shane and Ryan. They are incredible gifts of God to us. As a Christian father, when I started to read the Bible, it changed my heart and attitude. I have taught them God's Word, and now I pour into my grandchildren godly principles—awesome.

When a woman becomes pregnant out of marriage, the Christian in the relationship should take the responsibility of leading the child into a personal relationship with Jesus. Also, continue to lovingly lead the other person to the Lord, whether they eventually marry or not. The most important thing is that they know God and live in obedience to His Word. They are the other parent who will always be involved in the child's life.

In desperation, many couples choose to have an abortion. Choosing to end the life of a baby is murder. God commands in the Ten Commandments: *You shall not murder* (Exodus 20:13). Why should an innocent baby pay for the sexual sin that people commit? The baby is a living being—a soul. God forms a living human being in His image within the mother's womb; He breathes His breath into the baby. It is important that we understand what the Bible teaches about life. It is horrible to think of how many young adults are murdering their children. Millions of babies have been murdered in America—horrible.

A HEAVY PRICE TO PAY

It was only after I came to the Lord that I really began to learn what marriage was all about. I studied what a husband and a wife should be doing in a marriage and how to raise children. By the grace of God, His divine intervention, and persevering to be obedient to God's Word, God made our marriage work. It was all God's doing.

I still tell young people to be careful who they date, because there is no guarantee the person will come to the Lord, and even if he does, you may end up paying a very heavy price. I am speaking from experience and from God's wisdom. We reap what we sow: *Do not be deceived, God is not mocked; for whatever a man sows, that he will also reap* (Galatians 6:7).

Christians may look at our story and say, "Look, you were unequally yoked, and it has worked out for you!" Yes, the Lord has worked everything for good, just as Paul said in Romans 8:28: *And we know that all things work together for good to those who love God, to those who are the called according to His purpose.* However, for a long time, we lived hell on earth. I was making money and working hard, but I was very abusive and an adulterer. Sharon paid a heavy price for her choices for many years.

The mistake people often make is to be led and controlled by their flesh—carnal desires—and not by the Spirit. I am not only speaking from Sharon's and my personal experience. The Bible warns us by using the same lesson in the lives of great men and women of God, who were anointed by God and set apart to be used for His purpose.

The term *unequally yoked* has great meaning to us, yet this term did not begin with the teachings of Paul. It began way back in the Old Testament. The Lord commanded the children of Israel through Moses not to intermarry with the heathen nations around them, because He knew they would be influenced into idolatry:

> *"Take heed to yourself, lest you make a covenant with the inhabitants of the land where you are going, lest it be a snare in your midst . . . (for you shall worship no other god, for the LORD, whose name is Jealous, is a jealous God), lest you make a covenant with the inhabitants of the land, and they play the harlot with their gods and make sacrifice to their gods, and one of them invites you and you eat of his sacrifice, and you take of his daughters for your sons, and his daughters play the harlot with their gods and make your sons play the harlot with their gods."*

EXODUS 34:12, 14–16

When Israel left Egypt, God told His people not to engage in harlotry with the idols of the foreign nations who surrounded them. Later in history, Ezra reminded the people of God's command, when they returned to Jerusalem after being in captivity. There were many foreigners among Israel, and Ezra knew God did not want His people to marry their sons and daughters:

> *'Now therefore, do not give your daughters as wives for their sons, nor take their daughters to your sons; and never seek their peace or prosperity, that you may be strong and eat the good of the land, and leave it as an inheritance to your children forever.'*

EZRA 9:12

It is important to know that this was God's command from the beginning. He did not change His mind from the Old Testament to the New Testament. He knew His people would not follow Him if they married the people who worshiped foreign gods.

That is exactly what happened to Solomon. Even though he was the wisest man alive, and he knew better, Solomon married many foreign women, and they turned his heart from the LORD:

> But King Solomon loved many foreign women, as well as the daughter of Pharaoh: women of the Moabites, Ammonites, Edomites, Sidonians, and Hittites—from the nations of whom the LORD had said to the children of Israel, "You shall not intermarry with them, nor they with you. Surely they will turn away your hearts after their gods." Solomon clung to these in love. And he had seven hundred wives, princesses, and three hundred concubines; and his wives turned away his heart.
>
> 1 KINGS 11:1–3

Solomon's sin with foreign women became known throughout Israel, not just during his reign, but it is written in the Bible for us to read. The children of Israel knew Solomon's wives lured him away from God and that he had sinned against the LORD. They knew the command of God in Exodus 34.

Nehemiah, who was called to rebuild the walls of Jerusalem, spoke of Solomon's sin when he exhorted the children of Israel concerning being married to heathens:

> So I [Nehemiah] contended with them [children of Israel] and cursed them, struck some of them and pulled out their hair, and made them swear by God, saying, "You shall not give your daughters as wives to their sons, nor take their daughters for your sons or yourselves. Did not Solomon king of Israel sin by these things? Yet among many nations there was no king like him, who was beloved of his God; and God made him king over all Israel. Nevertheless pagan women caused even him to sin."
>
> NEHEMIAH 13:25–26

These exhortations and warnings were not only for the children of Israel. They are for every one of us who call ourselves Christians. We need to be careful about our intermingling with nonbelievers. If we enter any type of relationship with someone who is not walking according to the Spirit of God, we risk walking with them in the sin.

When Christians enter into relationships with nonbelievers, they always think they are strong in the Lord, thinking they can draw them to Christ, and they would never walk away from Him, but they are wrong. So many Christians backslide from these relationships. They get dragged back into the world, and there is a real danger they will not return to the Lord.

PLAYING WITH FIRE

Samson was a great man of God. He was a gift from the LORD to his parents in their old age and to the people of Israel. His birth was announced by the Angel of the LORD, who came to his mother and father to tell them they would have a baby in their old age. He would be the deliverer of Israel:

> And the Angel of the Lord appeared to the woman and said to her, "Indeed now, you are barren and have borne no children, but you shall conceive and bear a son . . . And no razor shall come upon his head, for the child shall be a Nazirite to God from the womb; and he shall begin to deliver Israel out of the hand of the Philistines."
>
> JUDGES 13:3, 5

Samson was anointed by God to be a judge of Israel and was given divine strength when His Spirit moved upon him (Judges 13:24). He became a mighty warrior and killed a lion with his bare hands (Judges 14:5–6). He caught three hundred foxes, set their tails on fire, and released them into the camp of the Philistines (Judges 15:4–5). Samson killed a thousand men with the jawbone of a donkey (Judges 15:14–17). He ripped off the gates of the city of Gaza, carried them 45 miles, and dropped them on the top of a hill (Judges 16:1–3). All these things he did with the anointing of God—with the strength of the LORD.

Samson was anointed by the Holy Spirit to serve the LORD and deliver Israel out of the hand of the Philistines. He was to be consecrated to God from his mother's womb, to the day of his death. The vow of the Nazirite required him to abstain from wine, never cut his hair, and avoid defilement by touching any dead corpse (Numbers 6:1–21). He was to be separated unto God, and yet Samson always associated with nonbelievers, married a heathen, and sought out prostitutes. Chosen to be God's vessel, the Spirit of God occasionally came upon him to accomplish God's work. However, he constantly yielded to his anger; he sought revenge and yielded to sexual passions. You could say, Samson had one foot in the world and one foot with the LORD.

Most Christians know the story of Samson and Delilah, a heathen Philistine. Yet Delilah was not the first woman to cause Samson to give in to his flesh. Even though he was a vessel of the LORD—set apart for Him—Samson had a big problem with lust. He should have married a woman from Israel, and he knew it, but instead, he looked to the world for a wife:

> Now Samson went down to Timnah, and saw a woman in Timnah of the daughters of the Philistines. So he went up and told his father and mother, saying, "I have seen a woman in Timnah of the daughters of the Philistines; now therefore, get her for me as a wife."
>
> JUDGES 14:1–2

Samson was a believer, empowered by the Holy Spirit. He was chosen by God and blessed by God. He had godly parents who knew Samson's decision to marry a Philistine woman was wrong. So they tried to talk him out of it:

> *Then his father and mother said to him, "Is there no woman among the daughters of your brethren, or among all my people, that you must go and get a wife from the uncircumcised Philistines?" And Samson said to his father, "Get her for me, for she pleases me well."*
>
> JUDGES 14:3

Samson's parents gave him godly advice, but he ignored them and followed his carnal desires, rebelling against the Word of God.

Listen, whenever we want to do something that goes against God's Word, we are in sin. Period. Nothing we choose over God is ever right. It is wrong and it will cause us harm. We have to listen to the godly people the LORD puts in our lives, especially when we allow our emotions to control our actions. We have to know and love God's Word more than the things of this world so we do not rebel against God.

Samson went to Timnah and spoke with the woman. He was very attracted to her, and he convinced his parents she was the one he wanted to marry; so, his father went to the woman and the Philistines welcomed him:

> *So his father went down to the woman. And Samson gave a feast there, for young men used to do so. And it happened, when they saw him, that they brought thirty companions to be with him.*
>
> JUDGES 14:10–11

They had a feast to celebrate the marriage, but the Philistine men had a problem with Samson. He gave them a riddle to solve. They became angry when they could not figure it out, because they would have to give Samson 30 linen garments and 30 changes of clothing. They did not want to lose, so they went to Samson's wife to make her find out the answer to the riddle (Judges 14:12–15).

Samson's wife was not loyal to him. She was loyal to her people. Instead of telling Samson what the men were trying to do, she went along with them and schemed to get the answer to the riddle:

> *Then Samson's wife wept on him, and said, "You only hate me! You do not love me! You have posed a riddle to the sons of my people, but you have not explained it to me." . . . Now she had wept on him the seven days while their feast lasted. And it happened on the seventh day that he told her, because she pressed him so much. Then she explained the riddle to the sons of her people.*
>
> JUDGES 14:16–17

Samson trusted his unfaithful, heathen wife, and she betrayed him to the Philistine men. Samson was so angry, he killed 30 men to provide the clothes the Philistines had won, and then he returned to his father's house. He left his Philistine wife behind, and she was given to his best man (Judges 14:18–20).

At this point, you would think Samson would have learned his lesson about getting involved with women from other nations, but he did not. He continued to pursue ungodly women.

Then, in the Valley of Sorek, Samson again sinned against the LORD by going into a Philistine harlot—Delilah. Samson was not walking in the Spirit when he chose this heathen woman over the LORD. Just like his first wife, the lords of the Philistines asked Delilah to betray Samson. She was very eager to do it because she was worldly, sensual and willing to betray him for money:

> *And the lords of the Philistines came up to her and said to her, "Entice him, and find out where his great strength lies, and by what means we may overpower him, that we may bind him to*

afflict him; and every one of us will give you eleven hundred pieces of silver."

JUDGES 16:5

Again, Samson should have seen the obvious warning signs because Delilah was just like his former wife. She acted in the same way, but Samson, led by his lust, became blind to her schemes: *So Delilah said to Samson, "Please tell me where your great strength lies, and with what you may be bound to afflict you"* (Judges 16:6).

Time and time again, Delilah tried to entice Samson to tell her where his great strength lay. Samson told her many things that would bind him and make him weak like any other man: bind him with bowstrings, new ropes that were never used, or weave his seven locks of hair into the web of the loom. Even though the Philistines rushed in every time to try and take him captive, he always broke free. He treated the situation as a game (Judges 16:6–14).

Finally, Delilah's constant nagging got to him, and she broke through his will. Samson told her all his heart:

> *Then she said to him, "How can you say, 'I love you,' when your heart is not with me? You have mocked me these three times, and have not told me where your great strength lies." And it came to pass, when she pestered him daily with her words and pressed him, so that his soul was vexed to death, that he told her all his heart, and said to her, "No razor has ever come upon my head, for I have been a Nazirite to God from my mother's womb. If I am shaven, then my strength will leave me, and I shall become weak, and be like any other man."*
>
> JUDGES 16:15–17

Now Delilah had Samson right where she wanted him. She called for the Philistines, who paid her in full for her betrayal. When Delilah had lulled him to sleep, she had a man shave off his hair from his head. Then she began to torment him (Judges 16:18–19).

The Spirit of the LORD departed from Samson, his strength had gone, and he was left to his fate with the Philistines:

> *And she said, "The Philistines are upon you, Samson!" So he awoke from his sleep, and said, "I will go out as before, at other times, and shake myself free!" But he did not know that the Lord had departed from him. Then the Philistines took him and put out his eyes, and brought him down to Gaza. They bound him with bronze fetters, and he became a grinder in the prison.*
>
> JUDGES 16:20–21

Look at the great cost of Samson's disobedience to the LORD. He was captured by the Philistines who bound him and plucked out his eyes. He no longer had the strength of the LORD. He was truly reaping the consequences of the life he had sown in the flesh. God had given him over to his lust for idolatrous women who did not know God. They did not love God, and they did not love Samson. They were subject to themselves and the world.

When the Philistines gathered together to celebrate and to offer sacrifices to their god Dagon, they praised their god for the capture of Samson—the destroyer of their land—the one who had killed so many of them. When their hearts were merry, they called for Samson to perform for them and be mocked in their temple. About three thousand men and women watched from the roof. Samson was stationed between the pillars of the temple, so he asked the lad who led him to put his hands on the supporting pillars (Judges 16:23–27).

When Samson cried out to the LORD—as he repented in his heart—God heard him. Thankfully, God is faithful, even though people are not. The LORD gave him the strength to defeat his enemies who had him in chains:

> Then Samson called to the Lord, saying, "O Lord God, remember me, I pray! Strengthen me, I pray, just this once, O God, that I may with one blow take vengeance on the Philistines for my two eyes!" And Samson took hold of the two middle pillars which supported the temple, and he braced himself against them, one on his right and the other on his left. Then Samson said, "Let me die with the Philistines!" And he pushed with all his might, and the temple fell on the lords and all the people who were in it. So the dead that he killed at his death were more than he had killed in his life.
>
> JUDGES 16:28–30

At one time, God had used Samson's life for His purposes. God had a great plan for his life, a perfect plan, but Samson chose his own fatal plan instead. Samson died with his enemies, but despite his failings, Samson also died as a hero of the faith (Hebrews 11:32).

The life of Samson was a great tragedy because he had a noble beginning, but a sad ending. We always think of Samson as being strong, but he was weak when it came to resisting temptation. His physical strength did not come from him; the Bible tells us the power he received was from the Holy Spirit. When he confronted the enemy, he would be filled with the Holy Spirit, and he could defeat them. However, when he was tempted, he did not depend on the LORD and gave in to the temptation.

Samson liked playing with fire; he liked adventures, and he paid a great price for them. Anytime you play with fire, sooner or later, you are going to get burned. He knew the Spirit of God was upon him, yet he would go and lie with prostitutes. He presumed upon the love and grace of God.

If you date out of God's will, you are playing with fire, and you will get burned. The nonbeliever is used to living like hell. When the believer is trying to convert someone who is living according to the world, it will rarely work. That is only the work of the Holy Spirit.

This is a great lesson to each one of us. Satan knows what temptation to put in front of us to cause us to turn from the LORD. The story of Samson is here as an example. There will always be temptation which can lead to lust while on this earth, so we need to train our eyes and our hearts to stay on the LORD and not on the things of this world.

Though Samson was called to be a judge for God's people, he dishonored God and lost his sense of judgment because he was not in tune with God. He was not obeying God's commands, praying, or in communion with God's people. He was taking advantage of God's grace—God's unmerited favor towards sinners. He lost touch, spiritually speaking, with God. He was doing his own thing.

Satan was watching Samson, just like he watches you and me. We have to be careful. Satan is after us and wants to set us up. Satan has bait, like fishermen. He will try to get you when you are down and weak. He will get you good when you choose to serve your flesh instead of serving God. There will be consequences, and they could be great.

A GOD OF PEACE, GRACE AND MERCY

While Samson chose to be unequally yoked, just like many men and women today, there are some Christians who are living in divided relationships, and it was not their choice. Many times, people get married while they are still in the world, and if the husband or the wife comes to the Lord, at that time, they become spiritually incompatible.

There are also some Christians who married in the Lord; the man and the woman were both walking with God, but one of them walked away. They are not united in their Christian walk with God anymore. They became unequally yoked. Again, they did not start out that way.

Being in a marriage with someone who is not walking with the Lord can be very difficult, but it is not an open door for divorce. This is when the believing husband or wife has to go back to the two greatest commands in marriage—love one another and submit to each other.

However, there is a time when a spouse can leave because of physical or severe emotional abuse, infidelity, or if they are keeping you from serving the Lord.

Paul has something to say for Christians who end up in broken relationships that were never their choice. To them he said this:

> *But to the rest I, not the Lord, say: If any brother has a wife who does not believe, and she is willing to live with him, let him not divorce her. And a woman who has a husband who does not believe, if he is willing to live with her, let her not divorce him.*

1 CORINTHIANS 7:12–13

God is a God of peace, grace and mercy. If you have been careless in obeying the Lord's commands by being involved in an unequally yoked relationship, know that He has a way of working in and through the situations of your life. He can turn any of your messes into something beautiful if you leave your mistakes in His loving hands for Him to fix.

Even if you have been left abandoned by a nonbelieving wife or husband, God wants to continue to use your life for His glory. He can make something good out of life's devastations. He is God—He does that! He will make your way to be peaceful and spiritually prosperous. There is always a future and a hope if you place God at the center of your life.

CHAPTER 7

SINS THAT RUIN A MARRIAGE

*Now the works of the flesh are evident, which are: adultery,
fornication, uncleanness, lewdness, idolatry, sorcery, hatred,
contentions, jealousies, outbursts of wrath, selfish ambitions,
dissensions, heresies, envy, murders, drunkenness, revelries,
and the like; of which I tell you beforehand, just as I also told
you in time past, that those who practice such things will
not inherit the kingdom of God.*

GALATIANS 5:19–21

God created marriage to be the most fulfilling relationship between a man and a woman, outside of a relationship with Jesus Christ. Marriage is to be protected, nurtured and sustained by God's Word. However, when a husband or wife fails to guard their marriage from sin, they allow the enemy to come in like a flood. If permitted, Satan will divide and destroy their marriage.

DIVISION

Every marriage will face storms—seasons that are rough and destructive. During these times, to avoid dissention, a husband or wife should first recognize that their enemy is Satan, who is seeking to destroy their marriage. They should not open the door for him to come in and cause division. Each should have a strategy to keep Satan out.

In the battle for a marriage, it is essential that the couple remain in the Word, obey it, and pray with each other. The only way they can defend their marriage against demonic attack is by keeping Christ at the center of their relationship; His wisdom and guidance are the weapons to overcome the enemy's assaults.

King Solomon understood the necessity of having God in the center of a relationship when he wrote: *Two are better than one . . . and a threefold cord is not quickly broken* (Ecclesiastes 4:12). A threefold cord has far greater strength than only two strands. For a marriage to be strong, Christ has to be the third cord—the third Person to strengthen the marriage.

A husband and wife must have the authority of Christ at the center of their marriage, so their relationship will remain united through the Spirit of God, not divided by each of their individual, carnal desires— the flesh.

Avoid division in your marriage by dying to self. As Christians, we are to live a life of self-denial; Christ instructs: *"If anyone desires to come after Me, let him deny himself, and take up his cross daily, and follow Me"* (Luke 9:23).

The Apostle Paul lived the crucified life; he wrote: *"I have been crucified with Christ; it is no longer I who live, but Christ lives in me; and the life which I now live in the flesh I live by faith in the Son of God, who loved me and gave Himself up for me"* (Galatians 2:20).

In our own strength, we will walk in the flesh, living for ourselves and thinking only of our own needs. If we do not learn to die to our self-life before we get married, we will have a hard time cleaving together to become one.

Christians need to know that when they seek only their way in their marriages, they will cause dissension. So they each need to yield to each other, submitting to one another in the pursuit of marital unity.

In every marriage, there will be disagreements, because every person comes into a marriage with certain ideas and expectations. People have certain learned behaviors and habits from their parents, others and life in general. They may continue doing those things, believing that this is the right way to conduct their marriage. It is sometimes hard to see things from a different perspective and to change, but if they are willing to be directed by the Lord and die to self, they can resolve any issue.

When you look at the character of Christ, you see a Man who humbled Himself to the Father and to mankind. He considered the needs of others before His own. We must follow His example, deny ourselves, and apply the same principle in our marriage relationships.

The Apostle Paul called us to unity in Christ:

> *Therefore if there is any consolation in Christ, if any comfort of love, if any fellowship of the Spirit, if any affection and mercy, fulfill my joy by being like-minded, having the same love, being of one accord, of one mind. Let nothing be done through selfish ambition or conceit, but in lowliness of mind let each esteem others better than himself. Let each of you look out not only for his own interests, but also for the interests of others.*

> PHILIPPIANS 2:1–4

And continuing, Paul used Christ as the model of humility for us to follow:

> *Let this mind be in you which was also in Christ Jesus, who, being in the form of God, did not consider it robbery to be equal with God, but made Himself of no reputation, taking the form of a bondservant, and coming in the likeness of men. And being found in appearance as a man, He humbled Himself and became obedient to the point of* death, even the death of the cross.

> PHILIPPIANS 2:5–8

In your marriage relationship, are you following Christ's example of humility? As a husband or wife, do you consider your spouse's needs before your own? When there is love, lowliness of mind, and genuine esteem for one another in a marriage, Satan will not be able to cause division.

If we are true followers of Christ, we will bear the fruit of the Spirit within our marriages: *But the fruit of the Spirit is love, joy, peace, longsuffering, kindness, goodness, faithfulness, gentleness, self-control . . .* (Galatians 5:22–23).

When you allow the fruit of the Spirit to grow in your life, you will lovingly talk openly with each other, you will have peace and unity in your marriage, and the fruit of the Spirit will be evident.

SELFISHNESS

Selfishness will cause contention in a marriage. If two people are going to be joined together for life, they must be willing not to insist on everything being done their own way. It is important to speak about what matters most to each of you and come to an agreement together. This does not mean a spouse will have to compromise their integrity or faith, but they do not allow something simple, like squeezing the toothpaste in the middle, to become an issue between them. Instead of fighting over something so silly, just buy two tubes of toothpaste!

When two people come together as one in an inseparable marriage union, each one can no longer think and act as a single person. The couple has to consider the other person's feelings and needs. You are no longer your own. You belong to one another and should treat your spouse as you want to be treated. Without the Lord, a husband or wife will become too selfish to truly love their spouse. God is not glorified by selfishness and arguments.

With that said, I believe a great tragedy found in marriages is for a couple to decide, for selfish reasons, not to have children. It could be because a couple wants material things—a house, a car—or they want to travel around the world. By doing so, they could miss out on what God intended for their marriage.

A marriage can become strained when either the husband or wife refuses to have a child. They become divided about the matter of children, and the issue creates a big conflict in the marriage. God's intent was for a man and a woman to marry and populate the earth—to have a family: *"Be fruitful and multiply . . ."* (Genesis 1:28).

Children are a gift from the Lord! I believe a husband and wife should use wisdom and pray concerning the timing to have children. I think it would be sad to have none. Why? Marriage is an intimate union God has gifted man with, so he can have the joy of having children and then grandchildren: *Children's children are* the crown of old men, *and the glory of children is* their father (Proverbs 17:6).

Be careful not to be consumed with your own selfishness. Consider the negative effects on your marriage due to social media, gaming and YouTube videos. Are you constantly ignoring your spouse while spending hours and hours on social media?

Yet another selfish problem stems from believing a husband or wife should meet each other's every need. Ruth Bell Graham gives wise advice concerning the misconception of such thinking:

> It is a foolish woman who expects her husband to be to her that which only Christ Himself can be; ready to forgive, totally understanding, unendingly patient, invariably tender and loving, unfailing in every area, anticipating every need, and making more than adequate provision—such expectations put a man under an impossible strain—The same goes for the man who expects too much from His wife.
>
> Ruth Bell Graham

It is vital to the survival of the marriage that a wife understands the call of God on her husband's life; otherwise, in pursuing her selfish ambitions, she will divert him into a life God did not intend for him and destroy him.

There have been occasions when a man or a woman was called by God to serve in ministry or even in missions, but after marrying a person whom they believed to be supportive, they found out later in the marriage that they were not in full agreement—sad. All because of selfishness, the call of God was quenched, the spouse unfulfilled, and God's work left undone.

ANGER AND BITTERNESS

Anger, bitterness, and even hatred in your hearts for your spouse will destroy your marriage. Paul exhorted the husbands in Colosse: *Husbands, love your wives and do not be bitter toward them* (Colossians 3:19).

It is possible that a wife, by some action or word, has done something to cause a husband to have outbursts of anger towards her and to harbor bitterness against her. The word *bitter* in Hebrew means "to embitter, be irritated, exasperate, render angry, be indignant." However, even though a husband may become annoyed by his wife, he is not to treat her harshly or unkindly; he is to continue to love her with the love of Christ.

The Apostle Paul understood the heart of man and knew the only way Christians could live together in peace would be to take on the character of the Lord. In his letter to the church in Colosse, he urged Christians to be like Christ: *If then you were raised with Christ, seek those things which are above, where Christ is, sitting at the right hand of God* (Colossians 3:1).

Paul gave Christians an analogy of a man putting off old clothing and putting on new garments. Christians were to *put off the old man*, who they were before Christ, and *put on* Christian virtues, *the new man*, who is being conformed to the image of Christ. First, Paul gave a list of sinful behaviors for them to put off:

> ... *anger, wrath, malice, blasphemy, filthy language out of your mouth. Do not lie to one another, since you have put off the old man with his deeds, and have put on the new man* who is renewed in knowledge according to the image of Him *who created him.*
>
> COLOSSIANS 3:8–10

Then Paul gave a list of what Christians should put on: *Therefore, as the elect of God, holy and beloved, put on tender mercies, kindness, humility, meekness, long-suffering* ... (Colossians 3:12).

When anger, bitterness and hatred begin to rise in the heart of a husband or wife toward the other, in obedience to God, they are to by faith, humbly *put on tender mercies, kindness, meekness,* and be *longsuffering* toward their spouse. A husband and wife must come together, having self-control in the controversy. As each person practices *longsuffering,* their hearts will be tender and loving towards their spouse.

Peter exhorted believers in the same way:

> *Finally, all of you be of one mind, having compassion for one another; love as brothers, be tenderhearted, be courteous; not returning evil for evil or reviling for reviling, but on the contrary blessing, knowing that you were called to this, that you may inherit a blessing.*
>
> 1 PETER 3:8–9

We are to put off the old man: ... *put on the new man who is renewed in knowledge according to the image of Him who created him* ... (Colossians 3:10). God will bless a couple's marriage when they live in obedience to His Word.

UNFORGIVENESS

Unforgiveness is a sin. It will slowly eat away at your heart until it wipes out your marriage. When a husband or wife deeply wounds the other spouse with their words and actions, they must be willing to forgive. Each of them should pray on how to apologize and the proper time to do it. It is crucial to rid one's heart of unforgiveness and to forgive, just as Christ has forgiven us: *bearing with one another, and forgiving one another, if anyone has a complaint against another; even as Christ forgave you, so you also must do* (Colossians 3:13).

Sharon and I have been through horrendous times that have caused unforgiveness in our hearts. I physically and verbally abused my wife and committed adultery. So many times I feel guilty because of what I have done to her. God has forgiven me, and I know that she has found forgiveness through Christ for me, but those things will hurt me for the rest of my life—I remember them.

Sometimes when I am lying in my bed, the enemy harasses my mind with these thoughts—he crushes me. The devil is the accuser of the brethren. Yet I know the grace of God. He gives me His grace, His unmerited favor, and His abundant love and kind mercy. Maybe you have committed similar actions against your spouse, and you also need the forgiveness, grace and mercy of God.

Understand, the devil wants to condemn you, but Jesus Christ has made you a new creation. In my marriage, I have had to learn how to say, "I am sorry." I have to know how to love my wife.

STRIFE

Satan seeks to destroy marriages through constant strife, conflict, fighting, arguing and rivalry. To combat strife, a couple must pursue the peace of God; they can agree to disagree and still love one another. In the love Christ has given to them, they will be able to overcome differences and come together in agreement. The love of God is the perfect bond that will unite a marriage together: *But above all these things put on love, which is the bond of perfection* (Colossians 3:14).

Without the unconditional love of God in your marriage, there will be no peace in your home, and no one will be happy. When there is peace, your family will be blessed. Peace only comes from the Lord: *Peace I leave with you, My peace I give to you; not as the world gives do I give to you* . . . (John 14:27). You must . . . *let the peace of God rule in your hearts, to which also you were called in one body; and be thankful* (Colossians 3:15).

Peace comes through allowing God's Word to sink deep into your heart, mind and soul, as Paul instructs: *Let the word of Christ dwell in you richly in all wisdom, teaching and admonishing one another in psalms and hymns and spiritual songs, singing with grace in your hearts to the Lord* (Colossians 3:16).

If we dwell in the Scriptures and *let* them become the wisdom we use in our daily lives, they will produce peace in our relationships. Paul encourages *whatever you do in word or deed, do all in the name of the Lord Jesus, giving thanks to God the Father through Him* (Colossians 3:17).

ADULTERY

Marriage is a holy union created by God. It is to be held in honor and respect. God created it for man and woman to enjoy loving intimacy. He also desired to bless them with children. God protected the relationship by joining them together as one in a holy, inseparable union.

Just as the Lord forbids fornication—sex before marriage, He condemns adultery—sex with a person other than your spouse. A married couple is not to engage in any intimate relationship with another person outside of their marriage—it leads to adultery. There is no room in a God-ordained marriage for another person.

According to God's Word, adultery is sin. In the Old Testament, God commanded: *"You shall not commit adultery"* (Exodus 20:14). Adultery was punishable by death: *The man who commits adultery with another man's wife, he who commits adultery with his neighbor's wife, the adulterer and the adulteress, shall surely be put to death* (Leviticus 20:10).

The intent of this law was to protect the sanctity of sexual intimacy in marriage against the sinfulness of the human heart in committing adultery. God called for the man and woman caught in adultery to be put to death. God is serious about the sacredness of marriage. People who lived under the Old Testament were judged for their sins under the Law.

While the penalty for adulterers was stoning to death in the Old Testament, in the New Testament, Jesus brought the principle of grace. Adulterers are no longer stoned to death, but adultery does bring spiritual death to those who choose to indulge their flesh and refuse to repent.

God in His great redemptive love and mercy shows us grace through Christ. However, we must not take advantage of the grace of God. Grace means we do not receive the punishment deserved for our sins. We have forgiveness—God's riches at Christ's expense. Christ paid the penalty for our sins on the Cross:

> *For everyone has sinned; we all fall short of God's glorious standard. Yet God, in his grace, freely makes us right in his sight. He did this through Christ Jesus when he freed us from the penalty for our sins.*
>
> ROMANS 3:23–24, NLT

We are living in a time when marriage is not honored. Even those who call themselves Christians are abusing God's grace and committing adultery! In the church, there are too many people who do not fear the Lord, so adultery is becoming commonplace.

I have heard of spouses who go to churches with the intent of finding a date. While their spouse is in one church, they are seeing a person from another church! It happens! I would advise those who are married, if your spouse is skipping church on Sundays, you had better know where they are!

So many Christian men and women have experienced an attraction to someone at work or the gym. When another man or woman is attempting to get close to you, realize that Satan uses these situations to break up a marriage—be careful. That is his goal!

If you are a Christian, you should live a blameless life. Those who are married should not be engaging in intimate conversations with someone they feel they are attracted to—it does not have a godly appearance and could lead to sin.

As a Christian, I do not go to breakfast or lunch with women, only my wife. Why? Someone could say, "I saw Raul Ries with another woman." Then what happens? I am no longer blameless. Seriously, think about your Christian witness and what could happen—people talk.

As I mentioned before, there are going to be times when a married couple is not getting along. There are a lot of lonely, married women who hate their husbands. Married men can come to the place where they want to be alone. Satan sees the opportunity and will bring along somebody else.

Before I came to the Lord, I hardly paid attention to my wife. I fell into adultery, and because of yielding to my fleshly desires, my family suffered, and I had to reap what I had sown.

When a husband or wife commits adultery, they are sinning against God and their own bodies:

> *Flee sexual immorality. Every sin that a man does is outside the body, but he who commits sexual immorality sins against his own body. Or do you not know that your body is the temple of the Holy Spirit who is in you, whom you have from God, and you are not your own? For you were bought at a price; therefore glorify God in your body and in your spirit, which are God's.*

> 1 CORINTHIANS 6:18–20

Adultery has a domino effect: it grieves the heart of God by breaking fellowship with him. It breaks up families and hurts the children—it scars them for life! There are many children who have been destroyed because of their parents yielding to adultery.

Those who willfully commit adultery will suffer severe consequences that come to those who disobey God. Stay away from adultery—it will wreck your marriage and family!

LUST

In order to really understand where adultery begins, we need to listen to what Jesus taught His disciples in His Sermon on the Mount—the Beatitudes. In Matthew 5:27–30, Jesus explained to them how adultery begins in a man's heart:

> *"You have heard that it was said to those of old, 'You shall not commit adultery.' But I say to you that whoever looks at a woman to lust for her has already committed adultery with her in his heart."*

> MATTHEW 5:27–28

Jesus was referring to the Law, one of the Ten Commandments: *"You shall not commit adultery"* (Exodus 20:14). Jesus taught His disciples this major principle: a married person does not have to participate in the actual act of sex to be guilty of adultery. If they have lust in their heart, they are guilty of the act.

When a person entertains lust in their heart, they open the door for an adulterous relationship. Lust will eventually lead to the physical act of sex. One must not fall into the trap of thinking adultery is just a little flirtatious affair or simply an unattached, physical act. Adultery has serious consequences; unrepented sin can lead to eternal damnation (1 Corinthians 6:9).

In the reality of our world, with the advancement of technology and social media, temptation is everywhere. Sex is everywhere. No one is immune to Satan's ploys to tempt them. We can all relate to the problem of lusting. We are living in a fallen world, and there is so much sexuality around us. Sex sells, but we have to make the choice to resist the temptation and not give in to it.

Many people are addicted to sex—addicted to pornography and illicit relationships—while being married to someone else, and they do not have to leave their homes to get it. They can watch pornography and find all types of sex services online. Sexual deviation is at our very fingertips, making it easy to get and easy to hide from our spouses. While God calls us to be sanctified and set apart for Him, Satan does everything he can to cause us to give into the lust of our flesh:

> *For this is the will of God, your sanctification: that you should abstain from sexual immorality; that each of you should know how to possess his own vessel in sanctification and honor, not in passion of lust, like the Gentiles who do not know God . . .*
> 1 THESSALONIANS 4:3–5

Sanctification is the opposite of lust. Sanctification builds up the inner man, as he seeks to become conformed to Christ, while lust tears man down, leading to unholy living. Sanctification draws people closer to God and His Word, while lust causes people to do wickedly: *For of this sort are those who creep into households and make captives of gullible women loaded down with sins, led away by various lusts,* (see 2 Timothy 3:1–6).

Clearly, when we look at the Scriptures, submitting to lust is destructive to the soul. Unfortunately, there have been many men and women of God who have submitted to lust and have become bound by it. They should have been following the Lord, keeping their hearts and minds on God, but instead, they let down their guard—they were ensnared.

I have spoken with many people in the church who have committed adultery. I ask them these questions: How can you sit and hear the Word of God and knowingly be in an adulterous relationship? Are you convicted by the Holy Spirit? How can you grieve the Holy Spirit? The Holy Spirit dwells in every Christian, so a man and woman cannot commit adultery without feeling shame and guilt. Adultery cannot be hidden from the Lord. Always remember, the Holy Spirit convicts. God is watching, and He knows our sin. He sees everything.

DAVID AND BATHSHEBA

Adultery is a trap that even great men of God failed to avoid. King David and King Solomon, both father and son, were ensnared as they yielded to lust.

David, the King of Israel, a man after God's own heart, fell into sexual sin—adultery. His downfall is described in 2 Samuel 11–12. David was home relaxing, and he had not gone out to battle. One evening, he saw a beautiful woman bathing on a rooftop. He looked once, then twice—he lusted after her. David inquired as to who the woman was. Her name was Bathsheba, and she was married to Uriah, a faithful warrior in his army. David sent for her, had intimate relations with her, and sent her home.

About three months later, David received a message that Bathsheba was pregnant with his child! David must have thought, "How am I going to get out of this situation?" Consider how you would feel if something like that happened to you.

Although David was King of Israel, the Law demanded his death. Here is where Satan went to work. He placed a thought in David's mind so he could cover his sin. If he could get Uriah to come home from the battlefield and sleep with his wife, then he could say, "Congratulations, you are having a baby!"

Yet no matter how hard he tried to cover his sin of adultery, none of his plans worked. As a last resort, he had Uriah carry a sealed note and deliver it to David's cousin Joab, the commander of Israel's army. The note read that Joab was to take Uriah into the heat of the battle and withdraw from him so that he would be killed—now that was murder! David had committed adultery, and it led to murder. He sinned greatly against the LORD. David thought, *mission accomplished*. In order to cover his sin, he married Bathsheba, assuming no one would know about his sin. But God knew!

David did not repent until the prophet Nathan revealed to him his sin. Adultery brought terrible consequences on David's family. God told David *". . . the sword will never depart from your house."* David and Bathsheba's child would be born, but he would die. There was constant war in his house, a son's betrayal—and his kingdom was torn apart.

Have you considered the terrible consequences that would happen to your family because of adultery? Adultery will bring pain, suffering, heartache and war into your marriage.

KING SOLOMON

God was gracious and gave King David and Bathsheba a son who would become the next King of Israel—Solomon. Against God's command, Solomon acquired 300 wives and 700 concubines. He lusted after many foreign women. Solomon sinned greatly before God. Solomon wrote about the consequences of giving into the temptations of sexual sin. He warned young men about the evil of the immoral woman:

> *For the lips of an immoral woman drip honey, and her mouth is smoother than oil; but in the end she is bitter as wormwood, sharp as a two-edged sword. Her feet go down to death, her steps lay hold of hell. Lest you ponder her path of life—her ways are unstable; you do not know them. Therefore hear me now, my children, and do not depart from the words of my mouth.*
>
> PROVERBS 5:3–7

The immoral woman may look beautiful and enticing, but if a man yields to lust, he stands to lose everything. Notice the end of the path she leads him on—it leads to death.

Solomon warned young men of the immoral path that ends in total ruin:

> *Remove your way far from her, and do not go near the door of her house, lest you give your honor to others, and your years to the cruel one; lest aliens be filled with your wealth, and your labors go to the house of a foreigner; and you mourn at last, when your flesh and your body are consumed, and say: "How I have hated instruction, and my heart despised correction! I have not obeyed the voice of my teachers, nor inclined my ear*

to those who instructed me! I was on the verge of total ruin, in the midst of the assembly and congregation."

PROVERBS 5:8–14

Even though Solomon indulged in sexual relations with hundreds of women, he fully acknowledged that God only intended sexual intimacy between one man and one woman. Solomon understood that marriage was a sacred bond. He continued in his advice to young men to be intimate with only one woman—their wives:

Drink water from your own cistern, and running water from your own well. Should your fountains be dispersed abroad, streams of water in the streets? Let them be only your own, and not for strangers with you. Let your fountain be blessed, and rejoice with the wife of your youth. As a loving deer and a graceful doe, let her breasts satisfy you at all times; and always be enraptured with her love. For why should you, my son, be enraptured by an immoral woman, and be embraced in the arms of a seductress?

PROVERB 5:15–20

King Solomon gave another stern warning about the seductress—an evil, adulterous woman. A man will pay a heavy price when he allows himself to lust after her and be seduced. He will get burned!

For the commandment is a lamp, and the law a light; reproofs of instruction are the way of life, to keep you from the evil woman, from the flattering tongue of a seductress. Do not lust after her beauty in your heart, nor let her allure you with her eyelids. For by means of a harlot a man is reduced to a crust of bread; and an adulteress will prey upon his precious life. Can a man take fire to his bosom, and his clothes not be burned? Can one walk on hot coals, and his feet not be seared? So is he who goes in to his neighbor's wife; whoever touches her shall not be innocent.

PROVERBS 6:23–29

Solomon warned young men devoid of understanding not to take the path that leads to the house of a seductress:

> *And there a woman met him, with the attire of a harlot, and a crafty heart. She was loud and rebellious, her feet would not stay at home. At times she was outside, at times in the open square, lurking at every corner. So she caught him and kissed him . . .*
>
> PROVERBS 7:10–13

This woman was not single or a prostitute; she was the wife of a rich man—an adulterous woman who was behaving as a harlot. While her husband was away on business, she went after young, naive men who did not know any better. She enticed them saying:

> *"Come, let us take our fill of love until morning; let us delight ourselves with love. For my husband is not at home; he has gone on a long journey; he has taken a bag of money with him, and will come home on the appointed day."*
>
> PROVERBS 7:18–20

At the end of her wicked path of lust and adultery was destruction. It seems as though Solomon is describing a young man who caught a venereal disease—promiscuity took his life!

> *Immediately he went after her, as an ox goes to the slaughter, or as a fool to the correction of the stocks, till an arrow struck his liver. As a bird hastens to the snare, he did not know it would cost his life.*
>
> PROVERBS 7:22–23

Listen and pay close attention to Solomon's final exhortation as he gave a more detailed warning about the destructive path of the adulterous woman:

> *Now therefore, listen to me, my children; pay attention to the words of my mouth: Do not let your heart turn aside to her*

ways, do not stray into her paths; for she has cast down many wounded, and all who were slain by her were strong men. Her house is the way to hell, descending to the chambers of death.

PROVERBS 7:24–27

Never play or flirt with sin. Do not live on the edge of committing adultery. It is a serious matter to break your marriage vows before God. Unless you repent and turn from your lust, the destruction that you will reap may never be reversed.

If you as a husband or wife are engaging in another relationship with someone other than your own spouse, I pray you would break off that relationship and return to your first love. Repent and get your life right! Go home and begin to love and be faithful to your spouse.

Instead of being miserable in marriage, couples need to rekindle the fire in their marriages. The best way to do that is on your knees. Pray and ask God to renew your marriage. If you are open to Him, God will do a new work and bring you closer to each other than ever before. God can restore your marriage.

God's will is for your marriage to be healed. If you listen to the Holy Spirit through God's Word and prayer, you will experience a true transformation in your personal life and receive blessings in your marriage—you will please the Lord.

CHAPTER 8

DIVORCE

"For the LORD God of Israel says that He hates divorce, for it covers one's garment with violence," says the LORD of hosts. "Therefore take heed to your spirit, that you do not deal treacherously."

MALACHI 2:16

The first few years of our marriage were disastrous. These were difficult days to endure. As a nonbeliever, time after time I fought aggressively with my wife. We quarreled regularly over my sinful life as a nonbeliever and her commitment to live the Christian life. Would there be an end to all this strife? I shouted threats of divorce at her. Sharon defiantly snapped back, "I am here to stay!" She knew God could work the impossible in our lives. Sharon was immovable; she had been taught her entire life to make her marriage work. The will and work of God in a marriage was the most important pursuit. She knew before God she would stay—vowed inseparable.

Humorously, Ruth Graham, when interviewed about her marriage to the late Billy Graham, said: "I did not think of divorce but I did think of murder!"

Seriously though, divorce is a controversial topic because it has become such a huge problem in the church. Christian couples are divorcing their spouses for any apparent reason, and this is a tragic mistake. Instead of asking for godly counsel, those in difficult marriages often obtain worldly counsel. The ungodly will not encourage a couple to work out their problems by seeking the Lord. Quite the opposite—they often advise, "Just get a divorce!"

People in society have varied opinions about marriage and divorce. Yet I am not concerned with man's beliefs about marriage and divorce; I am committed to teach what God has said in His Word. God hates divorce.

Divorce was never a part of God's original design. In the Old Testament, God rebuked the corrupt priests in Israel for their treacherous behavior against their wives:

> . . . *the* LORD *has been witness between you and the wife of your youth, with whom you have dealt treacherously; yet she is your companion and your wife by covenant. But did He not make them one, having a remnant of the Spirit? And why one? He seeks godly offspring. Therefore take heed to your spirit, and let none deal treacherously with the wife of his youth. "For the* LORD *God of Israel says that He hates divorce, for it covers one's garment with violence," says the* LORD *of hosts. "Therefore take heed to your spirit, that you do not deal treacherously."*
>
> MALACHI 2:14–16

God hates divorce. He abhors it. God created a *companion* for the man so he would not be alone. Divorce causes a man to be alone without his helpmeet. Marriage is a sacred covenant—a vow between a man, woman and God—not to be broken. God *seeks godly offspring*. A divorce causes emotional damage to children, and they often go astray. Divorce is an act of violence. It tears two people apart who God united as one.

SPLINTERS OF DIVORCE

Think about marriages you know that have been destroyed through divorce, and how the lives of everyone in the family have been impacted. No matter the cause for the divorce, children are the ones who suffer the most. They do not understand why their mother and father are no longer together. Children become confused and even angry. These are consequences of rebelling against God's sacred institution of marriage.

God intended marriage to be permanent. It would be like gluing two 2x4's together and placing them between a vice to dry, becoming one. They would be permanently attached—inseparable. If you attempted to pry the two pieces of wood apart, they would splinter, leaving holes and damaging both pieces. That is what divorce does to a marriage; it splinters families. It brings devastation to each spouse, their children, family members and friends.

I believe divorce has become a big problem in the church, because Christians are no longer setting themselves apart from the world. Instead, they have become just like the world—marrying and divorcing. Christian couples are running from the altar of God to the divorce court of the world.

Some Christians have been married twice, even three or four times. I knew a businessman who was divorced and remarried five times!

If Christians continue to divorce and remarry, they will be held accountable. They will have no excuse before the Lord because His Word is clear. God hates divorce. There is a lack of the fear of the Lord in many married couples' lives; a husband and wife must obey God's Word.

BIBLICAL GROUNDS FOR DIVORCE

There are some Christians who try to compromise God's Word concerning marriage and divorce. Usually it is because of their sinful and selfish desires. They think nothing of breaking the marital vow made before God to their spouse, only to seek to be with someone else. These are Christians who look for loopholes in God's Word, so they can do whatever they want without feeling any guilt.

Common excuses couples use to get a divorce are: "We do not love each other anymore," "we are no longer compatible" or "we have separate interests." These are phony excuses for destroying a marriage. God does not make mistakes when He brings two people together—we make mistakes!

Before any Christians think divorce is the only option, they need to learn what God has said in His Word about the blessings that come through marriage. Allow God to work in your lives by being obedient to His Word, so you will be a stronger, godly couple.

God, in His Word, has given the biblical reason for divorce—adultery. There are certain times when a spouse is cornered into a divorce because of man's sinful practices such as: abandonment, spousal abuse, pornography, child molestation and endangerment. These serious acts in a marriage would require a separation for the safety of the victim, which, in many cases, leads to a divorce. In these situations, a person always needs to make a righteous stand and choose to submit to God rather than man.

INSEPARABLE

After spending time in Galilee, Jesus came to the region of Judea. It was here that the religious leaders approached Jesus and questioned Him about the legalities of divorce. They were always trying to entrap Him with their inquiries: *The Pharisees also came to Him, testing Him, and saying to Him, "Is it lawful for a man to divorce his wife for just any reason?"* (Matthew 19:3)

In the Old Testament, God gave laws to govern marriage. The Pharisees adhered to these laws written by Moses in the five books of the Bible, known as the Pentateuch. Yet when Jesus was asked about marriage and divorce, He took the Pharisees right back to the book of Genesis, before the Law was ever given, (Genesis 1:27; 2:24), where God first ordained marriage:

> *He* [Jesus] *answered and said to them, "Have you not read that He who made them at the beginning 'made them male and female,' and said, 'For this reason a man shall leave his father and mother and be joined to his wife, and the two shall become one flesh'? So then, they are no longer two but one flesh. Therefore what God has joined together, let not man separate."*

> MATTHEW 19:3–6

Jesus confirmed God's intent for marriage; it was to be a permanent relationship. God joined a man and a woman together in an inseparable union—becoming one. Notice what Jesus said, *"Let not man separate."* Write next to this verse in your Bible, "Let no man divorce." Why? God has joined them together—nothing and no one can separate what God has joined together.

The Pharisees, knowing that Moses instituted laws concerning divorce in the Old Testament (Deuteronomy 24:1–4), questioned Jesus, *"Why then did Moses command to give a certificate of divorce, and to put her away?"* (Matthew 19:7)

The Pharisees did not want to hear what God had instituted in the book of Genesis. They were more interested in what Moses allowed because they were divorcing their wives for any small reason, such as too much salt in their dinner! They were so critical of their wives.

Jesus knew they intended to trap Him in an argument of opinions. He took them straight to the authority of the Scriptures and told them what God said: *"Moses, because of the hardness of your hearts, permitted you to divorce your wives, but from the beginning it was not so"* (Matthew 19:8).

Notice, Jesus knew the real reason they had divorced their wives. He spoke God's truth to the Pharisees. Moses permitted them to divorce, because of the hardness of their hearts—divorce was never God's perfect will.

This is a universal problem; men's hearts are hardened against their wives. Those who are having marital issues look to the laws of man and ignore what God has written in His Word. As long as the courts give them a divorce, they think they are free to go out and remarry, but that is unbiblical.

Jesus again emphasized to the religious leaders the biblical reason for divorce. They could divorce in the case of sexual immorality. The innocent person who did not commit adultery could legally divorce, and they were free to remarry. Jesus corrected their selfish thinking:

> And I say to you, whoever divorces his wife, except for sexual immorality, and marries another, commits adultery; and whoever marries her who is divorced commits adultery."
>
> MATTHEW 19:9

If a spouse chooses to divorce for any reason other than sexual immorality, and he or she remarries, according to God's perfect plan for marriage, they are guilty of being in an adulterous relationship. They may get divorced for other reasons according to the laws of man, but God does not recognize a relationship outside of their first marriage.

NO CONDEMNATION

The subject of divorce is difficult. The reason a person has divorced is between them and the Lord. I know that there are people who have had to divorce for grave and even dangerous situations in their marriages and families. I also realize some people were divorced before they became Christians, and Satan has condemned them for what they have done in the past.

However, God does not condemn anybody: *there is* therefore now no condemnation to those who are in Christ Jesus, who *do not walk according to the flesh, but according to the Spirit* (Romans 8:1).

When a person comes to Christ, as a new believer, he can ask God for forgiveness. As a Christian, he begins a brand-new life in Christ; *old things have passed away; behold, all things have become brand new* (2 Corinthians 5:17). If you have been through a divorce, and you remarry, I would say, stay married and do not divorce again—count the cost—make the sacrifices needed to remain married.

I had a friend who waited five years for his wife to stop committing adultery. For five years he did not date anyone else; he just waited. When she got married to her boyfriend, he moved forward and continued serving the Lord. Then God brought him a woman, and he got married. They are still married to this present day! God honored them. He honors marriage.

While God allowed divorce because of adultery, through forgiveness, Christian couples who have committed adultery can come together and work things out in their marriages. No matter the situation, as they submit to God and to each other, He can bring peace into their marriage. God can redeem and restore a marriage. It is all His miraculous work.

THE ADULTEROUS WOMAN

In the book of John is an incredible story of forgiveness and restoration. Jesus was teaching in the temple when all of a sudden, the scribes and Pharisees brought to Him a woman caught in the very act of adultery.

These religious leaders knew the Law; adultery was punishable by stoning. Both the man and the woman were to be put to death.

Notice, the religious elite only brought the woman to Jesus, but not the man. Both were guilty, but they only accused the woman in their attempt to bring a false accusation against Jesus' teachings. Would He contradict the teachings of the Law of Moses?

> *Then the scribes and Pharisees brought to Him [Jesus] a woman caught in adultery. And when they had set her in the midst, they said to Him, "Teacher, this woman was caught in adultery, in the very act. Now Moses, in the law, commanded us that such should be stoned. But what do You say?"*

> JOHN 8:3–5

Look at how Jesus responded to their scrutinizing question:

> *This they said, testing Him, that they might have something of which to accuse Him. But Jesus stooped down and wrote on the ground with His finger, as though He did not hear. So when they continued asking Him, He raised Himself up and said to them, "He who is without sin among you, let him throw a stone at her first." And again He stooped down and wrote on the ground.*

> JOHN 8:6–8

Jesus made a very powerful statement to the Pharisees; those who had no sin in their lives could cast the first stone at the adulterous woman. They stood firm to condemn her, but then wavered as they realized the intent of what Jesus had said. Could He have been writing each one of their sins on the ground? Those who stood in judgment of the adulterous woman were convicted as they walked away:

> *Then those who heard it, being convicted by their conscience, went out one by one, beginning with the oldest even to the last.*

And Jesus was left alone, and the woman standing in the midst.

JOHN 8:9

The accusers left, and the adulterous woman stood before Jesus alone. He had not allowed the religious leaders to stone her. As the Son of God, He too, could have judged her, but He did not—He showed her love, forgiveness, mercy and grace:

> *When Jesus had raised Himself up and saw no one but the woman, He said to her, "Woman, where are those accusers of yours? Has no one condemned you?" She said, "No one, Lord." And Jesus said to her, "Neither do I condemn you; go and sin no more."*

JOHN 8:10–11

Jesus did not condemn the adulterous woman—He forgave her. However, notice His one important exhortation, *"go and sin no more."* She needed to change and stop her adulterous, sinful ways. When any sinner has received the grace, mercy and forgiveness of God, there needs to be true repentance—a complete change.

FORGIVENESS

When a husband or wife is guilty of adultery, a spouse is biblically free to divorce and remarry in the Lord. At this point, a spouse may say, "I have biblical grounds for divorce. My spouse committed adultery, and I am out of this marriage!" Before a spouse makes a rash decision, they should stop and really consider what God has taught in His Word.

Yes, adultery is biblical grounds for divorce, but if there is true repentance, God would rather, there would be forgiveness if at all possible. Instead of divorcing, the innocent person can forgive the offending spouse, so they can be reconciled to their spouse through forgiveness (Ephesians 4:32; Colossians 3:12–13). God is faithful; He will guide an injured spouse in their decisions and bring them peace.

My wife had a biblical right to divorce me for committing adultery as a nonbeliever. Sharon, after an outburst of anger, chose to forgive me and allowed God the time to work in my life. She always felt in her heart that I would eventually get saved, and she wondered how God was going to use my life. When I came to Christ, I knew I was going to serve the Lord for the rest of my life. It was then that I made up my mind that I was never going to divorce my wife—ever. I realize I would not be alive today, preaching the Gospel, if it were not for Sharon, her sister, mother and father, and her grandpa and grandma, praying for me.

SEPARATION

The Apostle Paul recognized there would be times in a marriage relationship when problems occurred. During this period, he advised a time of separation. A couple could separate and give God time to work in their individual lives and in their marriage:

> *Do not deprive one another except with consent for a time, that you may give yourselves to fasting and prayer; and come together again so that Satan does not tempt you because of your lack of self-control. But I say this as a concession, not as a commandment.*
>
> 1 CORINTHIANS 7:5–6

It is important to understand what Paul was teaching in these verses. A husband and a wife are to be affectionate to one another; they are not to deprive one another sexually, except with consent, for a time of fasting and prayer. It is a time for healing and restoration of a marriage.

REASONS TO REMAIN MARRIED

The Apostle Paul wrote a letter to the Corinthian believers concerning the sanctity of the marriage as the Lord ordained it from the beginning:

> Now to the married I command, yet not I but the Lord: A wife is not to depart from her husband. But even if she does depart, let her remain unmarried or be reconciled to her husband. And a husband is not to divorce his wife.
>
> 1 CORINTHIANS 7:10–11

Paul addressed Christians who were already married to nonbelievers. Paul encouraged them to remain in their marriage relationship because of the incredible, spiritual influence they would have on the nonbelieving spouse and in their home:

> But to the rest I, not the Lord, say: If any brother has a wife who does not believe, and she is willing to live with him, let him not divorce her. And a woman who has a husband who does not believe, if he is willing to live with her, let her not divorce him. For the unbelieving husband is sanctified by the wife, and the unbelieving wife is sanctified by the husband; otherwise your children would be unclean, but now they are holy.
>
> 1 CORINTHIANS 7:12–14

Besides the fact that God hates divorce, Paul knew another good reason for them to stay together:

> For how do you know, O wife, whether you will save your husband? Or how do you know, O husband, whether you will save your wife?
>
> 1 CORINTHIANS 7:16

ABANDONMENT AND REMARRIAGE

In the Corinthian church, if a Christian was left by a nonbelieving spouse who never returned, the spouse had been abandoned. In such cases, divorce and remarriage was acceptable:

> *But if the unbeliever departs, let him depart; a brother or a sister is not under bondage in such cases. But God has called us to peace.*
>
> 1 CORINTHIANS 7:15

It is the same principle used today. If the nonbeliever has abandoned the marriage, a Christian believer is free to divorce and remarry. They are no longer in bondage to the marriage, because their spouse has forsaken and deserted them. Those abandoned can have peace of mind and heart. Understand, married couples will have disagreements, and one spouse may leave the house for a time to be alone. This is not considered abandonment.

We know we are living in the last days, and people no longer care about what God has instituted in the beginning about marriage. The world has redefined marriage, but marriage is clearly defined in the Word of God. No marriage can succeed without obeying it. That is why we see so many people divorcing and remarrying. They do not realize that they have been deceived by the world's view.

SPOUSAL ABUSE

There are so many marriages that are completely destroyed because of spousal abuse. God never intended for any woman or man to be physically, verbally or emotionally abused. God abhors any degree of abuse. A verbally abusive spouse will always tear down and never build up their mate. They always demean their spouse by calling them names, such as, "stupid" or "idiot" and other much more painful and profane words. A spouse or a child who suffers emotional abuse can be emotionally damaged for life.

A spouse may have a legal right to separate or divorce in extreme cases. However, God hates divorce. The abused person should seek the Lord in prayer and fasting, and consider how the abuse is affecting their Christian walk and the spiritual welfare of their family—their children. The spouse must consider the spiritual damage done to the children. A parent has been given a great responsibility; they have been commanded by God to bring up their children in the ways of the Lord. Parents need to protect their children and make sure they are not spiritually destroyed. It is possible they may grow up to be a victim of abuse or be influenced to become abusers.

The Lord has commanded us to love the Lord our God with all our heart, mind and soul. How is that possible if your mind is being harassed, and your life is restricted by continual abuse? Also, the abused must consider if their life and the lives of their children are in danger. For the emotional well-being and safety of the family, a spouse may have to seek a separation or a divorce.

However, there is always hope in the Lord for your marriage to work. Seriously, if you are going through tremendous battles that have pushed you to a breaking point with your spouse, I would encourage you to fight for your marriage on your knees! Be in prayer. Stick with it! Do not let the devil destroy your marriage.

As a husband or wife, humbly approach your spouse, despite your individual issues, and tell them you are sorry for whatever you have done wrong in the relationship. If you are on the brink of a separation or divorce, give God a chance to work in your lives—I beg you—please, please stay together.

God has given His counsel, not only for a marriage to work, but for a husband and wife to enjoy the blessing of a God-ordained marriage. His Word is foundational for a marriage relationship to be all that He intended for it to be. It is all there in the Bible—we just have to obey it.

CHAPTER 9

PARTNERS FOR LIFE

*Live joyfully with the wife whom you love all the days
of your vain life which He has given you under the sun, all your
days of vanity; for that is your portion in life, and in the
labor which you perform under the sun.*

ECCLESIASTES 9:9

How the years have flown by! As I reminisce, I cannot believe our marriage has endured for over 50 years. Sharon and I are still enjoying a partnership with an eternal purpose—the high call to serve God with our whole heart, mind, strength and soul. God has joined two very different people together as one. During our marriage, Sharon and I have kept a single passion, to be about our Master's business—to seek and to save the lost.

Some may ask, "What has been the secret to your marital union of over 50 years?" So simple—we have kept Christ at the center.

However, as much as I love my wife, most of the time I turn to the Lord for encouragement, not to her or anybody else. She does the same. I know Jesus will never fail me. Jesus knows me, He understands me, and He knows my heart. Though she might try to understand me, she cannot; she might be my wife for life and my lifelong friend, but there is no one like Jesus Christ.

Our lasting marriage has felt the brunt of many storms, the full force of satanic assaults, and life's sorrows; but through the grace and mercy of God, we have experienced great blessings and reaped such rich rewards. We are a Christian family, united in the love of Jesus Christ, surrounded by our children, grandchildren, and, if the Lord wills, our great grandchildren!

A marriage dedicated to ministry has enormous challenges and sacrifices. Sharon has been the right help-meet, the wife of my youth, my close companion, and the mother of my amazing three sons, Raul Jr., Shane, and Ryan. She has fought and endured life's battles, and stood faithfully by my side all these years.

Within our marriage is built an incredible trust that has allowed us the freedom to serve the Lord apart from each other. Sharon, like her missionary parents, Edmund and Naomi Farrel, has pursued her call for missions in South America. She has invested a lifetime in carrying on the vision of her parents of building and establishing Bible schools. Besides teaching God's Word and encouraging the nationals, I have watched how the Lord has used her life on the mission field tremendously. The Lord has given me the honor of planting churches and holding pastors' conferences throughout the entire region. Her parents laid the foundational work, and together we have continued to build a lasting legacy in South America.

When I look back over the years in ministry that the Lord has given to me, I think about the awesome privilege I have had to be personally taught by my pastor Chuck Smith and to preach the Gospel in Calvary Chapel. Millions of people across the world have heard the message of salvation through the *Somebody Loves You Crusades*, the *Somebody Loves You Radio*, and social media. The Lord miraculously provided for a movie of my life, *Fury to Freedom*, and several documentaries: *A*

Venture of Faith, *A Quiet Hope*, *Taking the Hill*, and numerous books—some still in the making. The fruit of this ministry has stretched far and wide—amazing—amazing! We have seen so many lives changed—a harvest of souls—only known by God. He alone gets all the glory.

Incredibly, I have met with Israel's President Benjamin Netanyahu and the King of Tonga. In England, I had the privilege of meeting with the well-known British evangelist, pastor, and author Alan Redpath; I developed a friendship with the late Reverend Billy Graham, his son Franklin, and countless other godly men and women. What ventures of faith! What awesome lives Sharon and I have had serving the Lord together!

MARRIAGES OF THE BIBLE

Over the span of human history, the Word of God has given to us examples of marriages to instruct us. In the following stories, two couples lived very different lives; they both faced trying times and perilous circumstances in their marriages. We shall be encouraged by them.

One couple had a blessed union—they served the Lord together. In the second marriage, one spouse suffered tremendously, having to endure wickedness due to the other spouse being in rebellion to God.

AQUILA AND PRISCILLA

Aquila and Priscilla, a Jewish Christian couple, had a strong, indestructible marriage. They were partners in life—in marriage and ministry. They were tentmakers by trade. Together they established churches from Turkey to Greece.

The Roman Emperor Claudius gave a declaration that expelled the Jews from Rome. By the divine will of God, the Lord used Claudius to move Aquila and Priscilla to Corinth where they met the Apostle Paul. I love the way God brought Paul and this unique, married couple together. It was through their trade, as Paul was also a tentmaker. Paul was all alone, and he needed all the support he could get. All three became partners, not only in their tent making business, but also partners with the Lord in His work.

As a couple, they became great, loyal friends to Paul, even to the point of willingly putting their lives on the line for him. The apostle wrote to the Roman believers about them: *Greet Priscilla and Aquila, my fellow workers in Christ Jesus, who risked their own necks for my life, to whom not only I give thanks, but also, all the churches of the Gentiles* (Romans 16:3–4).

Aquila and Pricilla were seasoned Christians, knowledgeable in the Word of God. They met Apollos, an incredible person, mighty in the Scriptures, but he had limited knowledge concerning Jesus Christ and the Holy Spirit. Aquila and Pricilla noticed his preaching was incomplete, as he only knew the baptism of repentance that was preached by John the Baptist. They gave Apollos further instruction about Christ and the baptism of the Holy Spirit. Aquila and Pricilla, as an exemplary married couple, became pillars in the early church. They had a great working partnership in their marriage. Aquila and Pricilla were united in business as tentmakers, united in the Word of God, and united in their love and care for the Apostle Paul and Apollos (Acts 18).

NABAL AND ABIGAIL

Many couples are not partners in their marriages and much less in their worship of God. Abigail was a woman unable to be united in any way with her husband Nabal. Though she was a woman who feared the LORD, most likely through an arranged marriage, she became married to an ungodly, harsh, drunken fool who was an extremely rich herdsman. The Word of God describes Abigail as a wise and beautiful wife. Even though in a wicked union, she chose to partner with God in her unbearable marriage, the management of her home, and ultimately in the affairs God had for Israel (I Samuel 25:2–3).

There are wise women like Abigail who are married to men like Nabal—fools. These men can be harsh and unloving. Women suffer tremendously under their lack of leadership and bad decision making. I can imagine them wondering, "Why did I ever get married?" I believe many remain in difficult and challenging situations, praying, trusting and longing for God to intervene and heal their marriages.

David, before he became king, along with his 600 loyal warriors, protected Nabal's servants and thousands of his flocks in Carmel, without asking for anything in return. As was the custom, David sent some of his young men to ask Nabal for needed supplies. He expected a graceful answer; surely he would show them kindness. Instead, Nabal, full of pride, treated them shamefully and insulted David's honorable character by calling him a runaway servant. Nabal, refusing to acknowledge the known fact that God had anointed David to be the next King of Israel, sent the men away empty-handed (1 Samuel 25:4–12).

After hearing about Nabal's harsh words from his men, David instantly became angry. He immediately instructed every man to gird his sword. Together they readied themselves to attack Nabal and his household (1 Samuel 25:13).

Abigail was unaware of the situation until approached by one of the young men. He told her the full account of what had transpired between Nabal and David's men. She knew her husband had acted foolishly and perceived David would be angry. Abigail, knowing God had chosen David to be the future king, feared God and set out to protect her husband, her household and the future king of Israel from acting rashly (1 Samuel 25:14–17).

A woman who is unable to partner with her husband because of his rebellion against God must unite with Him to bring about His purposes, and therefore protect her marriage and her family. If you have a husband who is not a believer or is a foolish husband like Nabal, you do not have to be a partaker of his sin. When it comes to the things of the LORD, you must obey God rather than man. Like Abigail, in humility and honor, you can lead your family to serve the LORD.

Abigail, knowing her husband's harsh disposition and that his life was in danger, aligned herself with God's will and did not tell Nabal about her secret mission. He never would have listened to her anyway. She quickly gathered all the supplies to give to David and his men and made ready to intercede before him, for the lives of her husband and household (1 Samuel 25:18–19).

She needed to appease David so he would not shed innocent blood and sin against God. In loving persuasion, Abigail tried to make him see that acting in anger to bring retribution against Nabal for his foolish words would stain his character as the future king.

Notice the humility of Abigail. She bowed down to the ground in humility before David. She even took the blame: *"On me, my lord, on me let this iniquity be!"* David took notice of her humble character. Abigail was not boisterous or insistent. She did not try to take command; she remained calm, meek, temperate—beautiful (1 Samuel 25:20–25).

When Abigail was before David, she spoke honestly and truthfully. She was straightforward and explained to him about her difficult marriage to a foolish husband. Though she sought to protect her husband's life, his servants and his entire household, Nabal did not regard Abigail as his wise companion in life. He failed to tell her about David's request for supplies. If she had known, she would have honored God, David and her husband by gathering the supplies for David's army.

In her humility, Abigail reminded David of his call. She knew of his integrity and how the LORD had fought his battles. Abigail gave David excellent counsel. She spoke common sense to David and helped him think through the actions he was determined to take. David did not need to damage his integrity.

Abigail also reminded David of God's presence in his life and gave confirmation about the promise of his kingship. She was a woman united in spirit with God, and her words cooled David's hot temper.

As Abigail spoke, David recognized her wisdom and knowledge were from the LORD. He blessed her greatly because he realized God had stopped him from shedding blood and from taking matters into his own hands. When Abigail finished her intercession, she asked David not to forget the good she had done in his presence.

Abigail may have recognized that God was still going to do something to judge her house because of her foolish husband Nabal. I believe she prepared herself for the worst. Yet God had a great plan for Abigail; He would honor her commitment to Him. David told Abigail to return home in peace—no harm would come to her household. Her family was spared (1 Samuel 25:26–35).

I thank God for my wife, because I know she has stepped in and interceded for me hundreds of times over the years. I could have acted rashly like David and made bad decisions. I believe husbands need to be able to listen to the wise words of a godly wife. Many men have become just like Nabal because they have refused to believe God united them as one in marriage; they fail to listen to the advice of their wives, and it has destroyed them.

If you are married to a godly, praying woman, why not sit down and communicate with her? It could be the Lord is speaking to you through her. As you seek the Lord in prayer, He will guide you to make decisions according to His will.

TIL DEATH DO US PART

After meeting with David, Abigail went home to a foolish, drunken husband, who was holding a great feast in his house—like the feast of a king. Abigail waited until the next morning when Nabal was sober to inform him of David's intent to attack their household and her intercession before David. Nabal was shocked. His heart became hard as a stone. He had a heart attack and went into a coma! Days later, in judgment, God struck Nabal, and he died. God removed Nabal from the earth.

Despite Abigail's daily, distressing circumstances because of her husband's rebellion against God, she acted very wisely. Notice, Abigail had the perfect opportunity to have her husband killed. She could have had David do her the favor of ridding herself of a very difficult husband, but she chose to do him good all the days of his life! Through this story, it is evident in her marriage to Nabal that she was protected by God as she partnered with Him to fulfill His purposes.

Once David heard about Nabal's death, he remembered Abigail, and he sent her a marriage proposal. From the first time they met, David was very impressed by Abigail's wise character and her fear of God. David desired her as his wife, because she was both wise and beautiful. She became united in marriage for the rest of her life to David—the King of Israel! God's will is so perfect—amazing (1 Samuel 25:36–42).

COMPANIONSHIP

It seems contrary to God's character that He would strike a man dead. However, though God is love, He is also the Just Judge who must punish sin. Nabal lived a life of rebellion against God, and He abhors rebellion. He stood in defiance against God's divine plan to put David on the throne of Israel. He was a foolish scoundrel, harsh and unloving, a husband undeserving of a wife such as Abigail.

In fact in the book of Malachi, the priests were reminded that they had lost the fear of God in their ministry to Him. They had no truth on their lips. Disobedience was in their hearts, so they walked in broken fellowship with God.

The priests had *one* Father—God. As men, they had *one* Creator. They not only dealt treacherously with one another, but in order to marry pagan women, they dealt treacherously with their wives. In divorcing their Jewish wives, breaking their vows before God and their marriage vows, they were guilty of committing serious sins. They had committed an abomination in Israel by making themselves *one* with foreign women. Yet God had made them *one flesh* with their Jewish wives. The covenant, the Law of God, was treated as nothing. This abhorrence would bring God's discipline on them. The LORD, in His anger against the corrupt priests' sin commanded the guilty to be cut off (Malachi 2:10–12).

The covenant of marriage was built on creation, intended for the good of the human family. A marriage relationship is a sacred union that God has created. The priests acted contrary to nature and to God's holy union of marriage.

After committing these sins, they came and brought gifts and wept at the altar. God detests those who have a pretense of worshiping Him. God would not put up with their hypocrisy and did not regard their offerings (Malachi 2:13). What was the underlining reason? The priests needed to understand the gravity of their abusive treatment towards their wives. The LORD said to the priests:

> *Because the LORD has been witness between you and the wife of your youth, with whom you have dealt treacherously; Yet she is your companion and your wife by covenant. But did He not make them one, having a remnant of the Spirit? And why one? He seeks godly offspring. Therefore take heed to your spirit, and let none deal treacherously with the wife of his youth. For the LORD God of Israel says that He hates divorce, For it covers one's garment with violence," says the LORD of hosts. "Therefore take heed to your spirit, that you do not deal treacherously."*

> MALACHI 2:14–16

From the beginning, God saw that it was not good that man should be alone; therefore, he created a helpmeet for him, a partner in life—a companion. We marry to have a companion, to have a partner for life that brings forth children.

What is a companion? The Hebrew word *companion* means: "a wife." Bible commentator Matthew Henry, in reference to this passage, describes in old English manner a man's companion as follows:

> Wives are . . . *the nearest to thee of all relations thou hast in the world . . . who had thy first affections when they were at the strongest, was thy first choice, and with whom thou hast lived long. Let not the darling of thy youth be the scorn and loathing of thy age. She has long been the equal sharer with thee in thy cares, and grief's and joys . . . as with a friend, and in whose company he should take delight more than in any other's . . . to whom thou art firmly bound . . . married people should often call to mind their marriage vows, and review them with all seriousness, as those that make conscience of performing what they promised.*

It is important to understand that you have been granted, by the Lord, a short period of time on this earth compared to eternity, to love and enjoy your wife—your companion. There will be no other time to do so, as the Scriptures reveal there will be no marriage in heaven. Jesus said, *For in the resurrection,* [in our new bodies] *they neither marry nor are given in marriage, but are like angels of God in heaven* (Matthew 22:30).

God created a unique opportunity for married couples to be blessed by their marriage union. Your time is limited with your husband or wife during your life on earth to show marital affection to your spouse. We often forget there is only one life to live—one wife or husband to enjoy life together with as loving companions.

The Scriptures give validity to the intimate companionship only to be found in a marriage relationship in Proverbs 18:2: *He who finds a wife finds a good thing, and obtains favor from the LORD.* Marriage is a good thing! A husband needs to be content with his wife. C. H. Spurgeon said: "Happy is the man who is happy in his wife."

Couples need to grasp that the only way they will have a peaceful, life-long marriage is if God is kept at the center of their relationship. A strong partnership exists when the husband takes care of his wife, and a wife has the best interest of her husband at heart: *The heart of her husband safely trusts her; so he will have no lack of gain. She does him good and not evil all the days of her life* (Proverbs 31:11–12).

Husbands and wives can walk side by side as *one* on earth, as loving companions, living a blessed life, enjoying each other. Can you imagine what a marriage would be like if a man and a woman obeyed all the principles found in God's Word concerning marriage? It would be a blessed union. They would live to attain all that God intended for their marriage to be on this earth. A married couple would be fulfilled in all that God desired for them. It is important not to miss out on or waste this time together. If you do, then when your spouse is gone, you will be filled with guilt and regret.

I admit, especially in my youth, I dealt treacherously with my wife. I was just plain mean to her. Besides that, I would never show affection toward her. She would have loved to have held my hand, but I have always been shy about showing affection in public. Even after I came to the Lord, I still did not take her hand. I have missed years of opportunity to show my love to her by this one, simple act of affection—holding hands. Now Sharon needs me to hold her hand at times, to steady her. I imagine the future, when Sharon is gone; I will never be able to hold her hand again.

In marriage, it is comforting to know we have a companion who is next to us. We are not alone. However, when your partner is taken from you, what happens? The person grieves; your most intimate friend during this lifetime is gone.

In wisdom, King Solomon summed up the importance of keeping God's commandments in marriage throughout one's entire life:

> *Live joyfully with the wife whom you love all the days of your vain life which He has given you under the sun, all your days of vanity; for that is your portion in life, and in the labor which you perform under the sun.*
>
> ECCLESIASTES 9:9

INSEPARABLE UNION

Now in this final season of life as close companions, Sharon and I, are growing old together. Over the years, there has developed a greater respect and sensitivity toward each other. We both have a strong desire to take care of each other. I feel concerned for my wife; her well-being is a priority, as she has been afflicted with cancer for over eleven years. You would never know it, as she serves the Lord still with such energy and determination. Her face is set as flint! Most people would be unaware of the tremendous battles she daily faces, but as her companion, I see, I know, and it is difficult to think of life without her by my side.

Humorously, Sharon desires for me to be taken home to be with the Lord first, because she is concerned over who will wash the sheets and keep the house in order! She wants to take care of me to the very end! We laugh more together, and sometimes cry with tears of rejoicing, for all God has done—this season of life is great.

When Sharon tries to tell me something, often I do not answer. Seriously, I do not hear her; I am not ignoring my wife. She has to raise her voice, because I am getting deaf in one ear. She is convinced I have selective hearing. That is what we argue about these days. Patience is needed toward the end of the race.

As we gracefully age, we talk openly and frankly about our final plans. There are fewer days before us than behind us. God has numbered them. We know our time together on this earth is coming to an end, and we look victoriously to the Author and Finisher of our faith as we face eternity.

As a couple, our companionship and conversations are important. We make a point to have breakfast at our kitchen table; numerous calls throughout the day help us to stay in touch with what each of us is doing. Our conversation is mostly regarding the exciting way God is moving in the ministry. Later in the day, like most ordinary people, we make dinner plans. On occasion, we both sit and watch an old movie together—unheard of in our past.

In our busy married lives, intricately woven together is our ministry and our family. We all serve the Lord! God is always on the move, and I know He is not finished with us yet. So we continue to walk a steady path, leaving behind us, with each step, a lasting legacy of enduring faithfulness, commitment and steadfastness for our children and grandchildren to follow in their marriages.

Our lives have been an open book for everyone to read. Though we have faced many trials in our marriage, we have this testimony before the witness of men, and more importantly, before God: Through His mercy and grace, Sharon and I are together, partners in life—*vowed inseparable.*

MARRIAGE VOWS

Biblical based vows that I use when performing a marriage.

THE BRIDES VOWS

I, _____, take you, _____, to be my husband so long as we both shall live. According to God's Word and with the help and guidance of the Holy Spirit I vow:

To love the Lord our God with all my heart, soul and mind (Matthew 22:37).

To spiritually adorn the hidden woman of my heart as the holy women of old, who trusted in God (1 Peter 3:3–5), and to love you and reverence you in the fear of the Lord (Titus 2:4–5; Ephesians 5:33).

To submit to you as unto the Lord; as the Church submits to Christ, and Christ submits to the Father in all things (Ephesians 5:22–24). To train up the children, that God may choose to give us, in the ways of the Lord (Proverbs 22:6).

To look well to the ways of our household by seeking God's counsel in all things (Proverbs 31:27).

Entreat me never to leave you or to return from following after you: for where you go, I will go; your people shall be my people, and your God shall be my God. Where you die, I will die, and there will I be buried. The Lord do so to me and more also, if anything but death part you and me (Ruth 1:16–17).

THE GROOM'S VOWS

I, _____, take you, _____, to be my wife so long as we both shall live. According to God's Word and with the help and guidance of the Holy Spirit I vow:

To love the Lord our God with all my heart, soul and mind. To love, nourish and cherish you even as Christ also loved the Church and gave Himself for it (Matthew 22:37; Ephesians 5:25).

To dwell with you according to knowledge, giving honor unto you, as unto the weaker vessel as being heirs together of the grace of life; that my prayers be not hindered (1 Peter 3:7).

To cleanse you by the washing of the Word that I may present you one day before Christ holy and without blemish. To be the head of our home even as Christ is the head of the Church and the Savior of the body (Ephesians 5:23, 26–27).

To provide for you and the children that the Lord may choose to give us, that I may be blameless before God. To follow wherever the Lord may lead that we may be always in His perfect will. In the presence of God and these witnesses I declare my vows to you.

SOMEBODY LOVES YOU PUBLISHING

BOOKS

Raul Ries

From Fury to Freedom
From Fury to Freedom***
Man: Natural, Carnal, Spiritual
Impurity: The Naked Truth
Sin: The Root of All Evil
Doctrines: A Simplified Road Map of Biblical Truth
Doctrines: A Simplified Road Map of Biblical Truth***
Servant: The Person God Uses
Victory: Overcoming the Enemy
Seven Steps to a Successful Marriage
Seven Steps to a Successful Marriage***
Raising a Godly Family in an Ungodly World
Somebody Loves You Growth Book**
30 Questions that Deserve Answers**
Understanding God's Compassion**
Living Above Your Circumstances:
    A Study in the Book of Daniel
Hear What the Spirit Is Saying

Chuck Smith

The Philosophy of Ministry: Calvary Chapel*

Sharon Faith Ries

The Well-Trodden Path
My Husband, My Maker
The Night Cometh: Edmund and Naomi Farrel
Written Bible Studies*

Claire Wren

Crimson

DVDs

Raul Ries

Fury to Freedom*
Taking the Hill: 2-DVD Package*
A Quiet Hope*
*A Venture in Faith: The History and Philosophy of the
    Calvary Chapel Movement**

SPANISH BOOKS & PAMPHLETS

El Pecado de la Ira
El Pecado de la Envidia
El Pecado de la Impureza
El Pecado de la Soberbia

SOMEBODY LOVES YOU ®
PUBLISHING
WWW.SOMEBODYLOVESYOU.COM

FILMS

Shane Ries

The Parisian Incident
Cycle
W 3sixty5
Abraham's Desert

Base 9
base9.com

*available in spanish
**booklet
***audio book

Somebody Loves You Radio is the teaching ministry of Pastor Raul Ries. Since committing his life to Christ in 1972, Raul has been driven to share the message of God's love to a lost and dying world on a 30-minute daily program which is heard worldwide on over 350 stations. It can also be accessed on the *Somebody Loves You* website, mobile app, and podcasts. The vision of *Somebody Loves You* is simple but powerful—to reach the world for Christ.